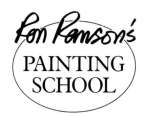

Drawing & Sketching

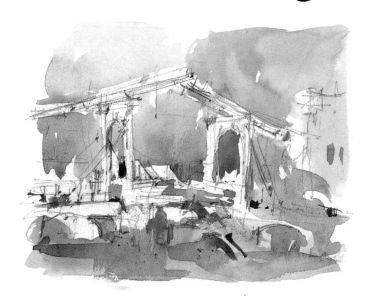

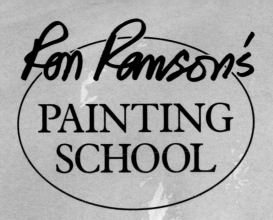

Drawing & Sketching

JOHN PALMER

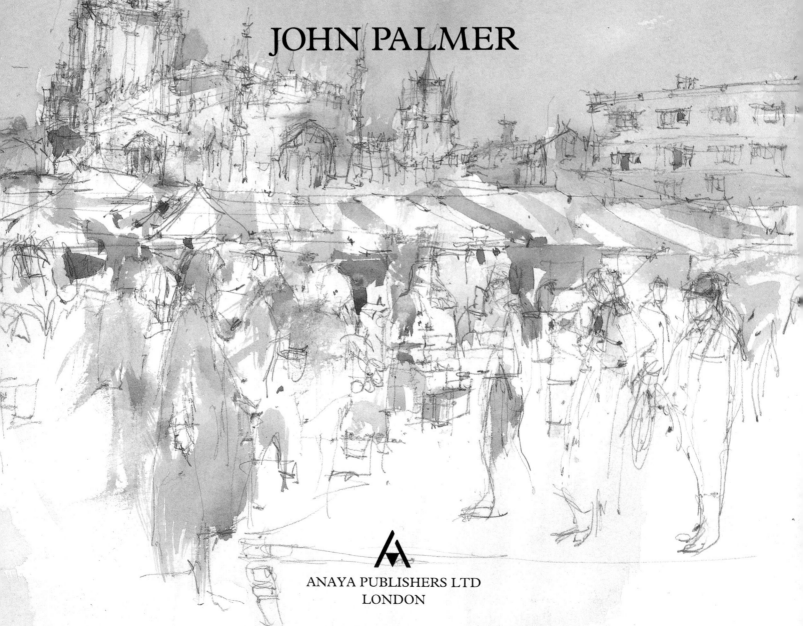

ANAYA PUBLISHERS LTD
LONDON

For Doreen – because!

First published in Great Britain in 1993 by
Anaya Publishers Ltd., Strode House,
44-50 Osnaburgh Street, London NW1 3ND.

Text John Palmer and Helen Douglas-Cooper
Editor Alison Leach
Art Director Jane Forster

British Library Cataloguing in Publication Data

Palmer, John
  Drawing and Sketching. - (Ron Ranson's Painting
  School Series)
  I. Title II. Series
  751.4

ISBN 1-85470-061-8

Typeset in Plantin in Great Britain by
Bookworm Typesetting, Manchester

Colour reproduction by J. Film Process, Bangkok
Printed and bound in Italy by OFSA Spa.

Front cover: Cornish Harbour.
Title page: Cambridge Market.

Contents

Foreword

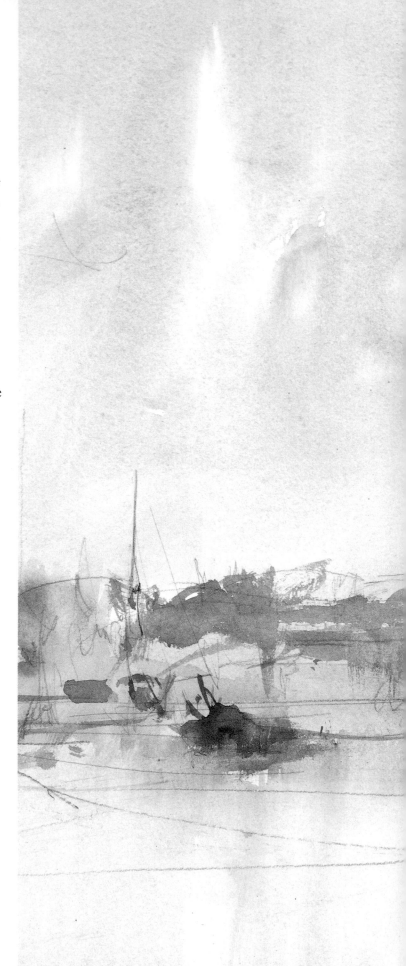

I have a huge library of art books at home and many of them are devoted to drawing and sketching. However, the illustrations in the majority look pretty anonymous – very efficient and workman-like, but it would be difficult to pick out a drawing from them and without a signature say 'so-and-so' did that; but John Palmer's work is different and when looking for an artist for this book, I knew he was the ideal person.

I had worked alongside him on countless Wednesday evenings at the prestigious Bristol Savages Club, whose members are mainly professional artists. The looseness and attack he put into his drawings and paintings astonished and thrilled me. Just watching him draw in his distinctive way made me want to emulate him. His pencil drawing just flowed effortlessly, or so it seemed.

He had had many exhibitions and his work fetched high prices but he had never ventured into writing a book himself although his work had appeared in other books. I managed to persuade him and this beautiful book is the result.

True to his character, he worked like a demon producing drawings and paintings that surprised even him. He can work in various media – pencil, charcoal, chalk, watercolour and gouache – sometimes using two or three in one picture. His subjects, too, are widely varied, from flowers to street scenes, but all done with this heady feeling of freedom and an unusual approach.

I hope his exciting work will persuade thousands of would-be artists to take up their various materials and have a go.

Ron Ranson

The scene was outlined in pencil, and very watery washes were added over it. The windmill was accentuated with touches of colour. The drawing of the windmill is quite tight, but this is balanced by the freedom of the brushwork in the surrounding scene.

Introduction

Drawing and sketching are one of the most individual ways of communicating your view of the world. In addition, places – and people – change over the years, and drawings can provide a personal record of your own life. They don't have to be outstanding, it is enough that they transmit moments and places in a memorable way.

Look for subjects all the time – around your home, at work, on holiday, even walking down the street. Draw things where you find them. You don't need a wonderful view in order to draw. Start by tackling the simplest subjects, drawing with pencil, and let this become second nature. When you feel confident, you can move on to more complicated approaches. If you have another interest – whether it is motor racing, sailing or gardening – combine that with drawing, because it is much easier to draw something you are knowledgeable about.

A drawing is finished when you decide it is, not according to a preconceived idea of completion. It is complete once you have recorded the information that you want or need. Many people go on working on a drawing beyond this point, losing the immediacy of the original statement. A drawing should contain its own history, so don't tidy it up.

It is important to show your work to other people, and to get honest reactions from them. You can always ignore what they say, but it will tell you whether you are getting across what you wanted to convey about the subject, and will also help others to share in your own vision of the world. Humour and enjoyment are important in drawings, and can be seen in lines that sing out from the paper. A drawing should be direct and spontaneous, not forced, and spontaneity develops through constant practice and observation.

Give yourself a time limit in order to generate some energy in a drawing. Such a limit also forces you to analyse what is important in the subject and to get that down quickly. Make several sketches of the same subject so that you get to know it. Try different mediums and approaches, and don't worry about making a mess. The important thing is to keep on producing drawings, and some of them will work. Others, when you look back on them in the future, will appear to have improved with age!

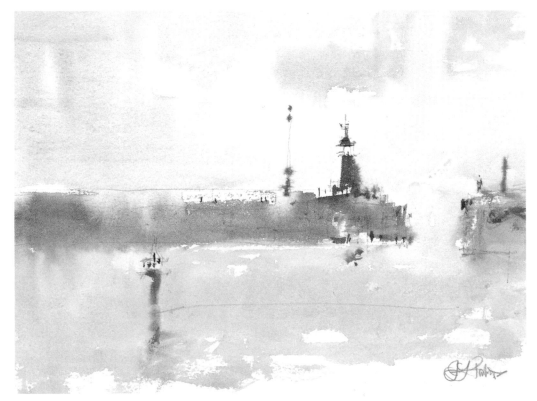

Watercolour was used to capture the atmosphere on the spot, working rapidly. To many this would appear unfinished, but it brings back memories of the occasion – five minutes of sunlight in an otherwise wet day. The sketch was done in that five minutes, concentrating on greatly simplifying the shapes of things in the scene.

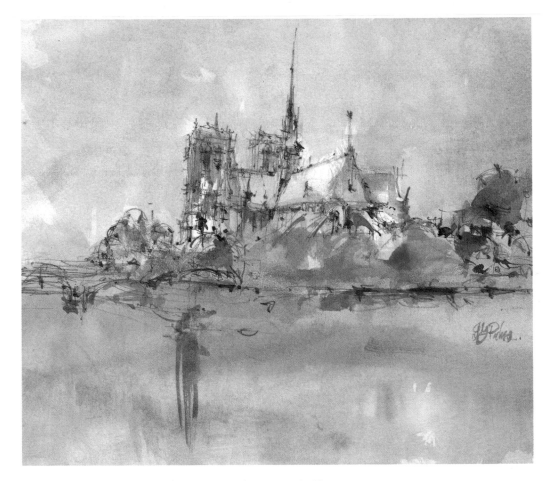

Pencil and wash were used over a tinted background. The washes were applied around the pencil work to isolate it, treating the pencil more as part of the overall colour scheme. The soft washes and integrated pencil line create a placid effect.

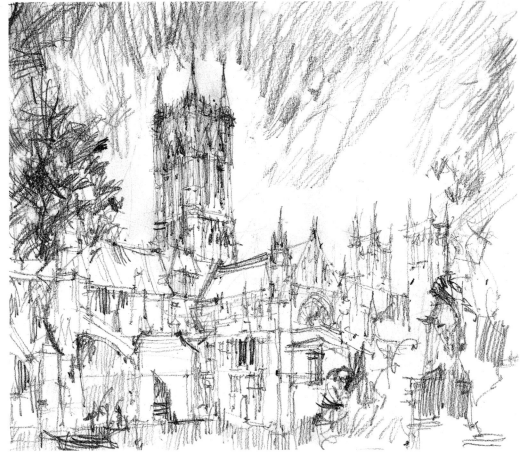

Although this is a static subject, the very vigorous use of line creates a sense of movement and energy, especially in the sky and trees. The building looks quite staid in contrast. This sketch was drawn very quickly, with no pauses until it was finished.

THE BASICS

Start by exploring different types of paper and materials. Don't necessarily set out to complete a sketch each time, just do enough to find out for yourself what they can achieve. Move on to a different approach if something doesn't work – it may just not suit your way of working, and anyway you can always come back to it later.

Once you feel confident with your materials, start exploring tonal effects. Whatever you are doing, try to keep within the bounds of the rules of composition, because this provides a strong basis for a drawing. If you want to incorporate colour, keep it simple.

A complex scene has been reduced to the main elements, rendered in pencil and wash. Vigorous lines and fragmented washes suggest life and activity.

Materials

PAPER

There are many different types of paper for drawing, including textured and coloured papers. Experiment with as many as possible to find out how they affect the materials you are using, and which give you the most satisfactory results.

CARTRIDGE PAPER

Cartridge paper is available in individual sheets and sketchbook form. Most cartridge papers have a smooth, silky surface, which enhances the quality of pencil lines – especially softer pencils. The smoother the surface of the paper, the greater the tonal range you can produce on it, whereas rougher surfaces create a broken line and make it more difficult to achieve a subtle gradation of tones. Washes on cartridge paper have a different effect to those on watercolour paper because the wash sits on the surface, resulting in a harder appearance, whereas on watercolour paper it is absorbed. Heavy cartridge paper is good for gouache.

WATERCOLOUR PAPER

Watercolour paper is available in a range of weights from 150 gsm (70 lb) to 600 gsm (300 lb). Those weighing up to about 400 gsm (200 lb) need stretching if they are to be used with water-based materials (page 36). Above that, the weight of the paper will prevent it cockling when it is wet. Lighter-weight papers are ideal for pen and wash; the heavier ones are better for watercolour.

Watercolour paper is also available with different surfaces: hot-pressed or HP (smooth), NOT (semi-rough), and rough. A smooth paper is best for pencil and wash. The advantages of a rough surface are that if you make a mistake, you can repeatedly remove what you have done and start again; and you can make a feature of the texture of the paper. Rough papers should only be used with paint, because the surface is too broken to use effectively with pencils or charcoal. Any drawing should be done with a brush.

It is possible to get tinted watercolour papers. These are useful for experimenting, because the highlights are dictated by the colour of the paper. Tinted paper can give unity to a sketch.

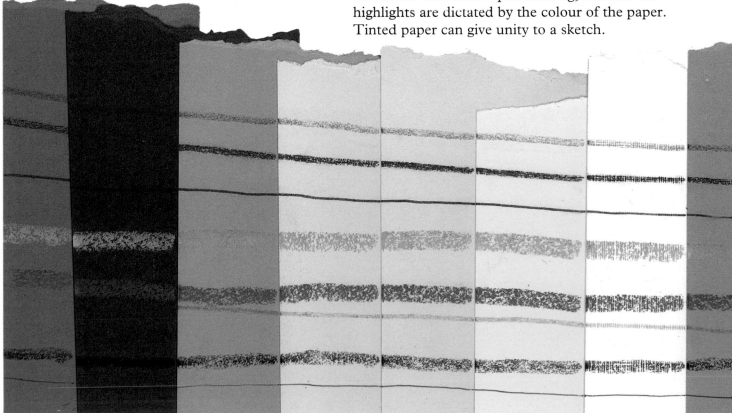

COLOURED PAPERS

Coloured paper can be used with charcoal, conté, pastel, gouache, acrylics, and some of the stronger wax crayons. Choose lighter-coloured papers for most materials, but the whole range can be used with pastels. A coloured paper gives unity to a drawing if it is allowed to show through in places.

A random selection of papers: from left to right, three examples of lightweight board, three examples of slightly textured paper, four examples of heavily textured papers, and two examples of very smooth, coloured papers. The drawing materials used on them are, from top to bottom: felt-tip pen, conté pencil, 2B pencil, soft pastel x 2, colour pencil, wax crayon and fine felt-tip pen. The pastels break up even on the smooth surfaces, emphasizing the texture of the paper and letting the colour show through. The fine felt-tip pen does not break up on any of the papers, even the heavily textured ones. The other materials emphasize the texture of the different paper surfaces to varying degrees.

OTHER SURFACES

Waste card – either from the back of sketchpads or from packaging – provides a cheap and wonderful surface for gouache, because the paint soaks in to create the same quality as a matt oil painting.

Textured paper, such as Ingres, helps you to achieve a range of effects with pastel, whether you are using the chalk on its side to block in large areas or making quick marks. However, even on smooth paper materials such as pastels can create texture. A textural effect is, therefore, not only dependent on the paper, but also on what you choose to draw with and how you use it.

Glossy board can be used with felt-tip pens, watercolour and gouache. It is difficult to work on but is worth trying as it can create some interesting blotchy, irregular effects.

Conté pencils used on two types of paper, the left-hand one a smooth paper, the right-hand one grained. It is possible to see the exaggerated grain on the rough paper although the same pressure of stroke was used across both papers.

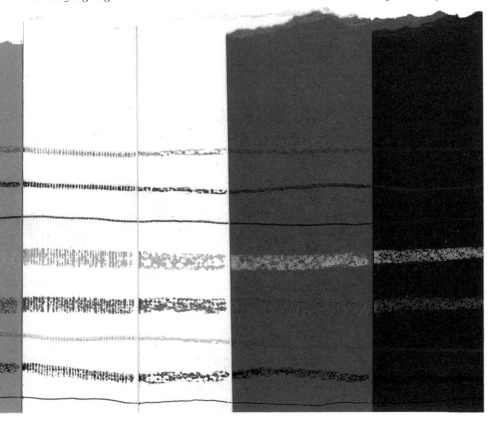

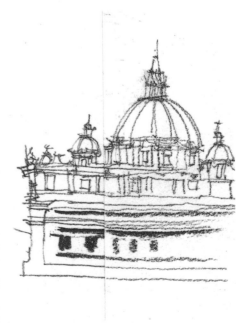

PENCIL

Once mastered, the pencil is a delightful medium because it can be used to create a wide range of effects. The great beauty of the pencil is that it can describe a form or shape with one line, and that line can vary between very light and very heavy. When you have become practised with a pencil, you will find it one of the most instinctive and enjoyable of all media to use.

Pencils come in a range of grades from very hard to very soft. The best grades for drawing and sketching are from HB (in the middle of the range), which is good for outlining the main shapes in a drawing at the start, to 9B (very soft), which creates the most dramatic effects. However, it is better to become accustomed to drawing with a harder pencil before trying a 9B, because you need to exercise a great deal of control and sensitivity with it. A 6B gives the largest range of effects from light to heavy marks and is best for general work.

USING LINE

Onc of the best introductions to using a pencil and finding out about its characteristics is to draw something like a flower, and keep drawing it again and again until you feel that the pencil has become an extension of your arm. Once you have got used to using a pencil, try drawing without lifting it from the page. Look at the shape of the subject, and then try and interpret it in one go using just line. Then see what effects you can get by using not only the point of the pencil, but also the side of a sharpened pencil, which gives a soft, grainy effect as you push it along. Try holding the pencil in different ways, which will also affect the character of your drawing.

When using pencil, it is not necessary to shade in every tone. You can use just line to give the effect of a shadow or shape. If the outline of an object disappears in an area of shadow, just let the outline disappear in your drawing, so that the edges are lost, by lifting off the pencil. This will give the impression of the edge of the form vanishing into shadow.

In all line work – whether in pencil or pen – confidence is important, because you've only got one chance to make a particular line. It is better to make a confident line that is slightly wrong, than a correct line that is too careful or tentative.

Right, six different pencils were used, from HB to 9B. The outlines were roughed in with an HB. A 2B was smudged under the bridge to create shadow, and was also used for the delicate details on the buildings. The texture of the paper was utilized for the shadow on the water by using a pencil on its side. In the top right corner, the soft, textured effect was created with a 9B. Some accents, such as the windows, were added to the left-hand building with a 6B, and the spire in the background and some accents in the sky were added with the 2B.

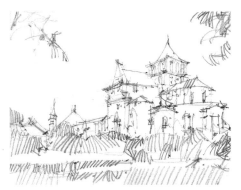

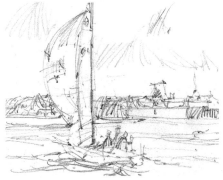

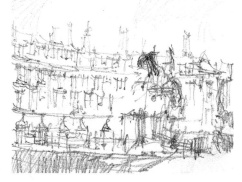

HB pencil. *First the buildings were lightly outlined, and then shading was added at the bottom. The pencil was used with different pressures – fine lines accentuate the edges of the buildings, broad marks suggest darker tones, and sharp, dark marks add accents.*

2B pencil. *A very light line was used to suggest cloud forms in the sky. The lines in the water describe the water surface. There is quite a contrast in the strength and range of marks achieved in this drawing compared to those in the drawing done with the HB pencil.*

3B pencil. *Fine lines were used around the tops of the buildings against the sky, and crosshatching was added at the bottom. Strength of tone was built up in the left-hand corner by working up layers of marks. Varying pressure was used to create a range of tones.*

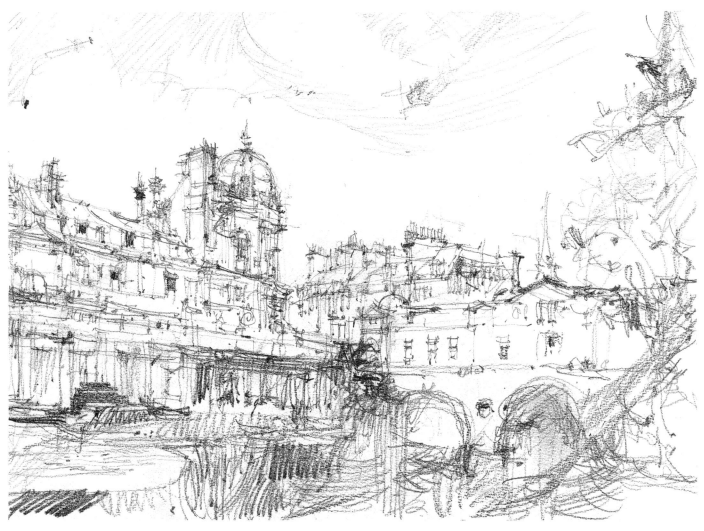

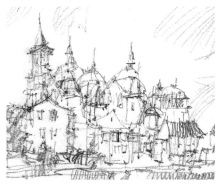

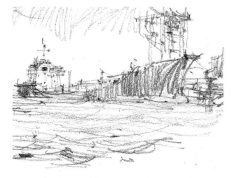

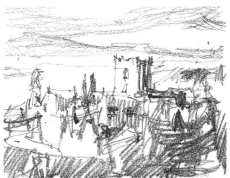

4B pencil. *The pencil is getting softer, and there is less contrast between this and the 3B drawing than, for example, between the 2B and the HB. A greater tonal range has been achieved with this pencil than with the harder ones, but the image is becoming less defined.*

6B pencil. *There is greater subtlety and broadness of marks with this than with the harder pencils. It exaggerates the texture of the paper, and the marks become broader and less well defined. Areas of pencil work become more solid, and there is less need to fill in details.*

9B pencil. *This pencil makes broad marks, and it is possible to build up a drawing very quickly. It also emphasizes the texture of the paper. The drawing was given a broader, heavier treatment, and there is great richness in the darker areas.*

PAPER

A pencil is affected by the surface that you are drawing on. In the beginning, use relatively smooth, lightweight cartridge paper, and play around until you achieve effects you like. Then you can experiment with rougher papers, and you'll see that with a rough, textured paper you need to be broader in your technique and create a simpler image, because the texture of rough paper breaks up the marks and makes detail impossible.

TYPES OF MARKS

The pencil can be used to make a wide variety of marks: line, broader marks with the side of the pencil, scribble, hatching, dots, smudging with the finger, and smudging and cleaning out with a rubber. Try to use as many as possible.

When used to describe a form, the lines can be curved to the contour of the form. Blocks of parallel hatching in different directions can denote various tones and shapes, and can add to the overall sense of pattern. Dots and scribble can be used to create texture in a drawing.

CREATING TONE

With a pencil there are two ways of building up tone. One is by using a soft pencil and creating the strength of tone you want through the pressure you apply as you draw. The other is by using a harder pencil and building up a series of tones by hatching in layers. However, bear in mind that often the most effective drawings are those that have had the least work done on them.

RUBBING OUT

In the beginning a rubber is essential because it allows you to experiment. Later on, you can use a rubber to remove or clean out areas of the drawing that interfere with the effect you want to create. If you leave in some wrong or unwanted marks, however, they can give a sense of construction to the drawing, and can give vibrancy to the edges of forms.

Right, this was done with an HB pencil, using a variety of marks to create different textures. Line was used for the shape of the trunk and the texture of the bark on the foreground tree, with parallel hatching in the direction of the slope of the trunk. Scribble was used to indicate the rough ground in the bottom right-hand corner. The tree in the background on the far left was first outlined lightly; then cross-hatching was added inside the outline to form the shape of the tree. Hatching in the left-hand foreground indicates the tufts of grass, and dots create a different texture on the ground against the tree trunk. Circular hatching around the branches indicates their cylindrical form. The solid area in the background indicates fields in the distance. Smudging creates shadows on the ground, and small, heavy touches of pencil all over the drawing create accents.

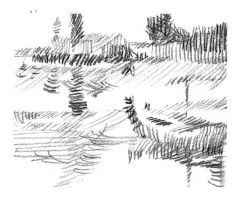

Parallel hatching can be used to create form and tone. Here it goes up to the outlines of the forms, but there are no actual lines around them – they are all created by areas of cross-hatching in different directions. The varying weight of the hatching creates different tones.

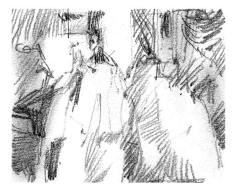

A combination of line and smudging. You can use line to create the shape or image that you want, and then add hatching where needed. You can then use a finger to soften the edges of the hatching slightly so that it isn't too dominant.

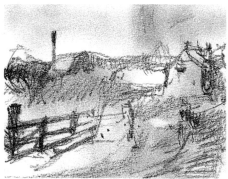

Tone was applied directly with the pencil, and the tonal range and quality were increased by smudging in some areas. Patches of white paper were left to create highlights, and the drawing was strengthened over the smudging in places. This creates a soft tonal effect.

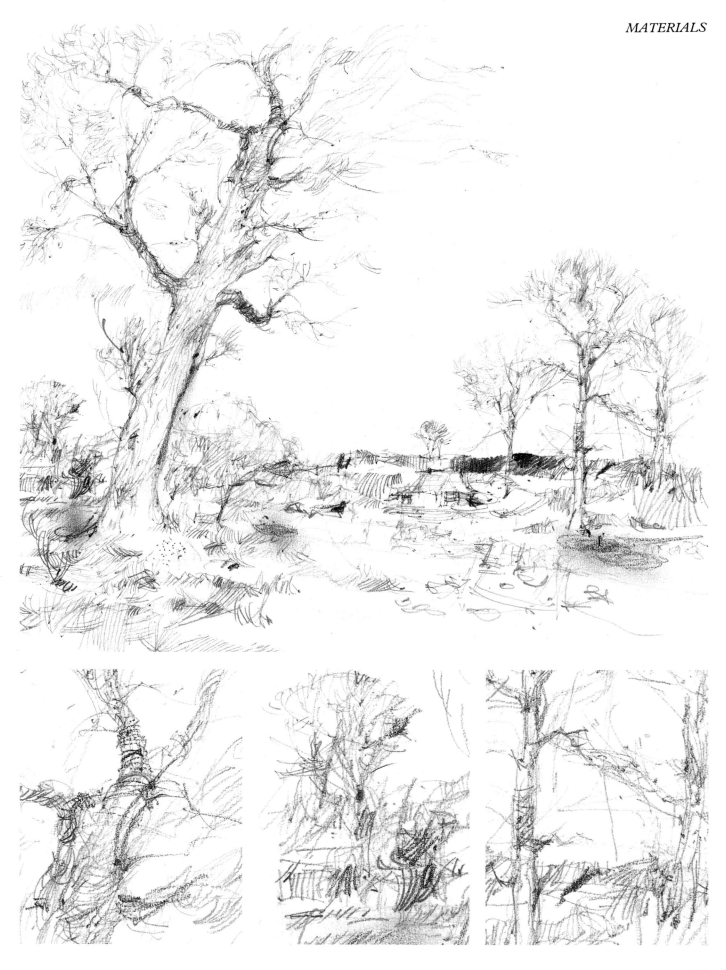

CHARCOAL

Charcoal is a very effective and interesting medium to use for drawing, and requires a bolder approach than pencil. It forces you to draw overall shapes rather than detail, and is most effective when it is used for broad, large-scale drawings.

There are two types of charcoal: willow and compressed. Willow is the more common. It gives softer, less intense tones than compressed, and is easier to move around and rub out. Compressed is darker and waxier, and is difficult to remove.

Charcoal makes a more permanent and direct statement than pencil, but don't let this put you off using it, because you can keep on working over a drawing and altering it until you have what you want. The rubber is far more important when using charcoal than with pencil. Because you are working in a broader way, you can add details with the rubber, and use it to clean out highlights. Charcoal drawings should be fixed to prevent them becoming accidentally smudged and ruined.

To begin with, use charcoal on smooth paper while you get used to the medium, but to get rich darks, you need to use it on a textured paper that will hold the charcoal well. Charcoal can also be used effectively on grey paper, letting the paper provide the mid tones. Darker tones are created with charcoal, and white chalk is used for highlights.

TYPES OF MARKS

You can use line, side of chalk, smudging, rubber, dots and scribble. Sticks of willow charcoal come in different thicknesses, which give different-sized marks. As it is used without sharpening, you can get broad, blunt marks. Used gently, possibly with some smudging, it can create subtle areas of tone. Drawings can be produced that are either consistently bold and heavy or subtle and soft; or that contrast soft shading with bold lines and marks.

When you are smudging charcoal, do it lightly in order to retain the texture and sparkle of the paper. One of the dangers of smudging is that it can make your drawing stylized if used too much. Think about why you are smudging, and use it with discretion.

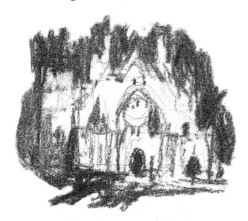

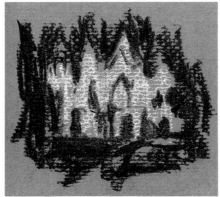

Far left, willow charcoal on white paper provides the maximum contrast. The image itself is quite soft.

Left, willow charcoal on textured grey paper. The grey paper provides the intermediate tones, charcoal the darker tones, and white chalk has been used for the highlights.

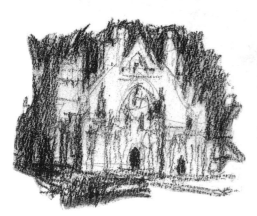

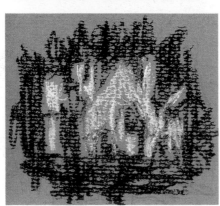

Far left, compressed charcoal on white paper. The harder, darker quality of the compressed charcoal increases the luminosity of the white paper, giving a more sparkling image.

Left, compressed charcoal on textured grey paper. It picks up more of the texture of the paper, giving a softer effect. The compressed charcoal gives a greater range of tones, but a less crisp image, compared to the willow.

Willow charcoal on white paper utilizing a range of effects: smudging, use of the paper's texture, heavier marks to get intensity, side of the charcoal in the foreground against smudging. The charcoal was used to create shadow areas without drawing. The counterbalancing of dark areas against light creates the edges of forms without a line being drawn, such as at the right-hand end of the boat.

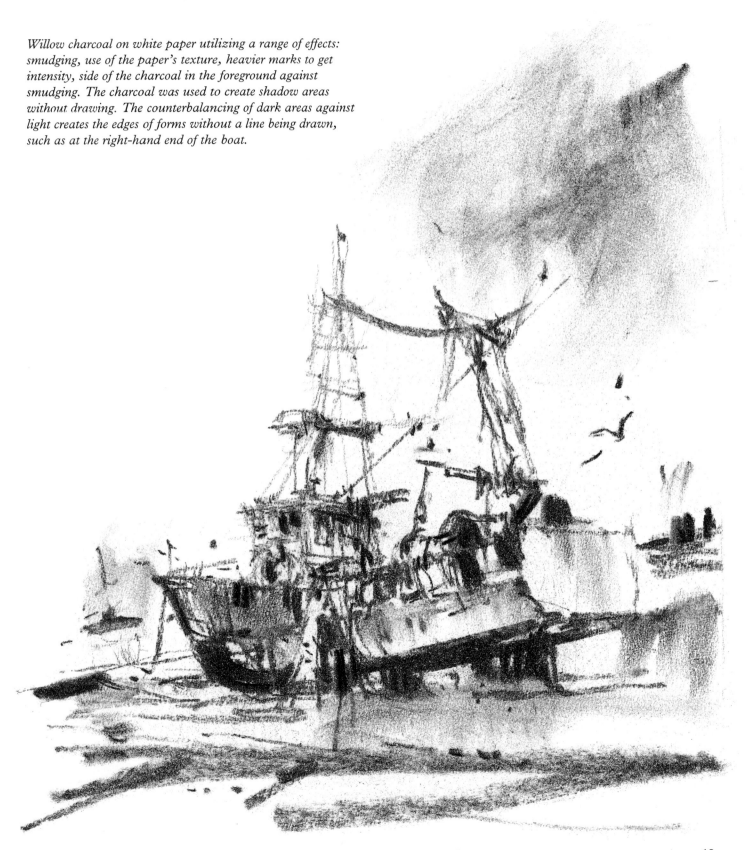

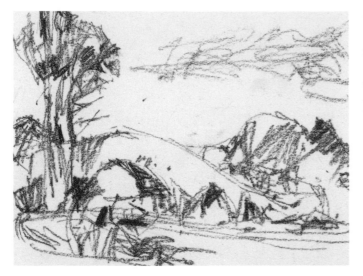

CONTE

Conté is one of the most attractive of all the monochrome materials. It has a pleasant tonal quality and colour, and is also very sensitive to the texture of the paper. It combines the advantages of pencil and charcoal because it can achieve line and texture in the same mark.

Conté is available as chalk – in square sticks – or as pencils. The advantage of the chalks is that you can use them in a broader and more dramatic way than pencils. A chalk can be used on its edge to create line, and on its side to block in areas of tone.

Pure drawing is possible with conté because tones are created by the pressure you apply as you draw. You don't build up areas of tone by hatching, for example, as you do with a pencil. A sense of unity can be easily created with conté because you don't need to use a wide range of different marks. It is best used by keeping the line going for as long as possible before lifting the chalk off, and by varying the pressure you apply in order to build up a greater intensity of colour for darker tones or accents.

Conté is compatible with coloured papers, especially lighter-toned ones such as cream and beige. Because it is very sensitive to texture, it should not be used on heavily textured papers as they will break up the marks too much. It is best used on its own rather than combined with other media because its strength lies in its singularity.

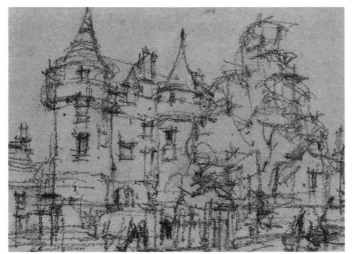

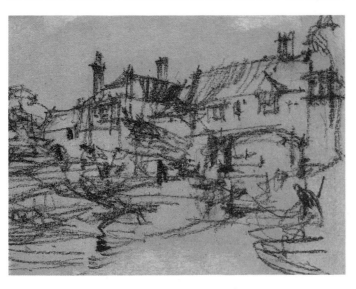

Top left, this was done in conté pencil on a cream background, taking advantage of the qualities and colour of conté. It was used very lightly in the sky, and more vigorously on the left-hand side in the tree.

Middle left, conté pencil used on a richer background, which gives a uniformity of colour. Because the background is a similar colour to the conté, a soft, harmonious effect is created.

Left, conté pencil used on a cooler, contrasting background. This gives the illusion of a stronger colour in the conté, and brings out the subtle differences in the weight of the marks.

Right, conté pencil on a cream background. The picture is dominated by the texture of the paper, creating tone on the top right-hand side. The pencil has been used to create a linear effect with a continuous line.

Far right, in contrast, the image is built up with blocks of tone, created using the side of the chalk.

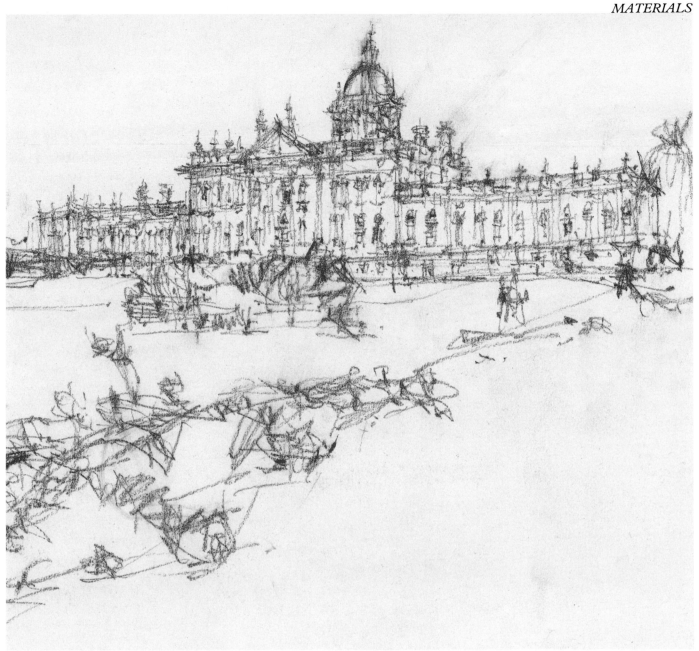

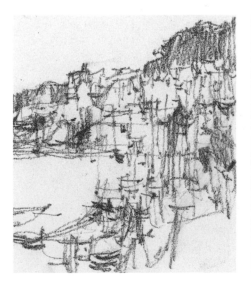
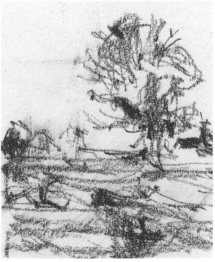

Above, conté pencil on cream paper. The drawing was built up with line, using vertical lines to construct the building, in contrast to the scribble in the foreground. The pencil was used with varying pressure from very soft to deliberately heavy. The soft marks have been used for details and in the background. Heavier marks have been used in the foreground, and to draw the viewer's attention to the dome on top of the building, the focus of interest.

PEN AND WASH

Pen and wash requires a very different approach from the previous materials. It involves very delicate use of line against something almost foreign to it – large areas of wash. Even the tightest illustrations can be loosened up with the application of a wash.

Fountain-type pens or felt-tip pens can be used for the line drawing, but felt-tip pens are best because they can create a continuous line, whereas re-filling or dipping a pen in ink can disturb the flow of the drawing. Some inks won't take washes, but lift off when a wash is applied over them, so make sure that you use a waterproof ink for the drawing. Washes can be watercolour, gouache or drawing ink.

If you have not tried pen and wash before, the best approach is to do the pen drawing first, and when complete apply the wash over it. Don't make the wash too intense for the quality of the line, or it will kill it. You need to strike a balance between what you see and what effect you want to create on paper, and this comes with practice. However, as a rule of thumb, on a large area you need to keep the wash a tone or two lighter than the tones in your subject. And bear in mind that a wash is usually stronger in colour and tone when it is applied than when it is dry. If a wash is applied to dry paper, it will have hard edges, whereas if it is applied to dampened paper it will have soft edges. When the wash is dry, you can assess whether you need to strengthen the pen line in places.

Generally, as with watercolour, a single wash is most effective, so you should try to avoid adding washes subsequently in order to adjust the first one that you put down.

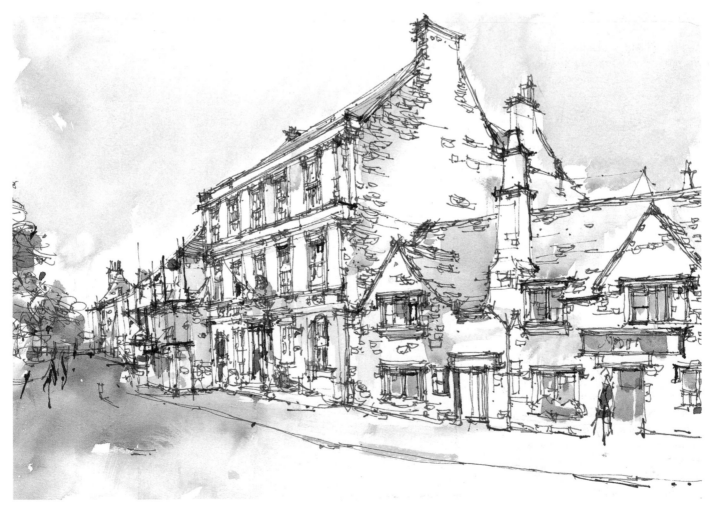

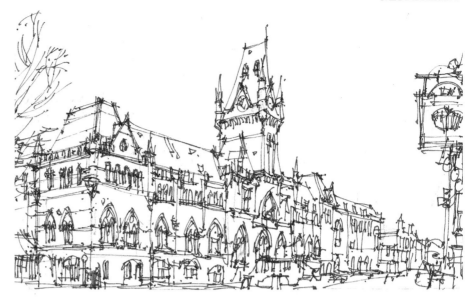

Line alone was used to create shapes and tones, and the varying strength of the line gives an impression of distance – it is heavier in the foreground and lighter in the distance. The drawing can stand without washes because of the composition and detail. Again, the windows were suggested rather than paintstakingly drawn in.

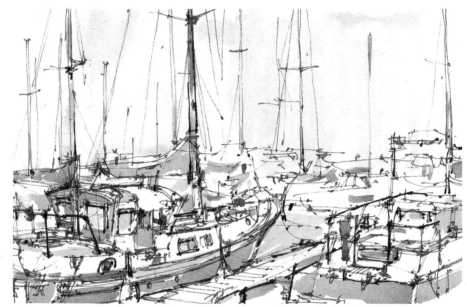

The pen work was done first. Not every mast has been drawn in; rather, an impression of masts has been created. The wash was applied discreetly, and the pen work was strengthened once it had dried. Much heavier lines were used in the foreground, to create a contrast with the distance.

This drawing of a woodland scene was done with a matchstick, sharpened and dipped in ink. It was used like a pen to draw line, and on its side. The strong marks were made first and as the ink dried, more delicate tones were added. The very soft, textural tones were achieved by using the matchstick on its side with slightly dry ink, together with some smudging with a finger.

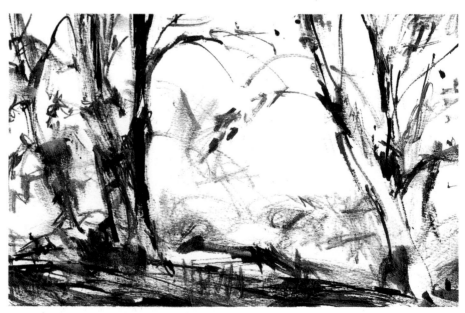

Left, the pen drawing was done first, and a wash applied over it. The wash doesn't always coincide with the lines around the forms; it is not necessarily used just to fill in areas of drawing. A number of details have deliberately been left out here, and small patches of white paper provide highlights.

Practice

It is well worth spending time practising with different materials. You can use everyday objects around the house, or simple scenes, as your subject. Keep on practising and experimenting with the different marks and effects that you can make until they start to become spontaneous. The examples here are to give you ideas for exercises in pencil, charcoal, conté, and pen and wash. You can also try combining these media, which will give you greater expressive scope. Water and marine scenes provide plenty of potential for using washes and trying mixed media.

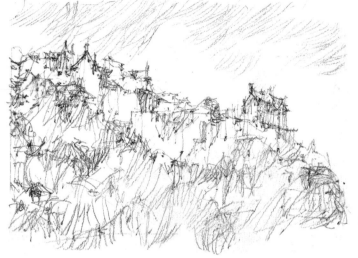

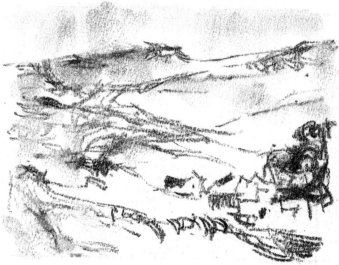

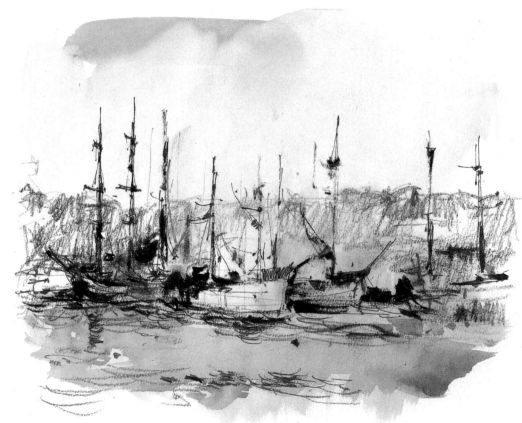

Above left, 4B pencil. When drawing with pencil, try to find ways to use line for building up tone as well as for creating the image. Vary the pressure on the pencil as you draw to give a sense of heavier and lighter tone, and add heavy accents with strong pressure where needed.

Above, willow charcoal. Combine line and smudge to create atmosphere and a sense of space, but do not specify anything in too much detail. Let patches of white paper show through.
 Try combining different media, such as pencil for light outlines, pen in the foreground, and a wash for the tonal areas.

Conté pencil on white paper. When using conté, concentrate on trying to achieve a loose but very active line, and keep the line going for as long as possible before lifting the pencil off the paper. Vary the pressure on the pencil as you draw in order to achieve variety in the line from light to heavy. Resist the temptation to shade in areas of tone.

When using a felt-tip pen, draw directly with it and work rapidly. Do not be tempted to do any pre-drawing in pencil. Don't worry about having a few lines or marks in the wrong place, because they will probably contribute to the overall effect of the finished drawing. You can add a wash if you think it is needed – try some drawings with and some without.

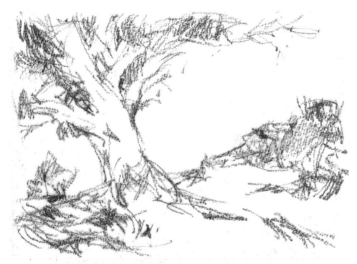

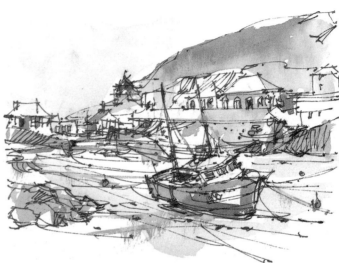

You can try mixed-media drawings using a variety of materials. This was done with conté in the sky, line work in pencil, light pen work accentuating the pencil lines, and gouache in the foreground. The colour in the foreground contrasts with the sky and exaggerated brushstrokes create texture.

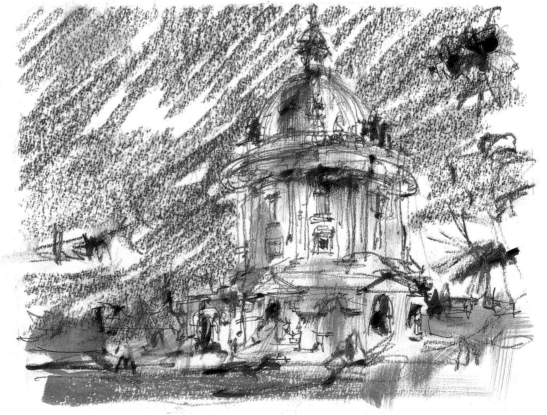

Colour Materials

A range of colour materials is available for drawing, such as colour pencils, felt-tip pens, pastels and wax crayons. In addition, paints such as watercolour and gouache can be used. You can build up a drawing using colour as line or using blocks of colour. You do not need to use colour realistically. It is better to select about three colours for a drawing and to use these in a schematic way – for example, one colour for light tones, one for medium tones, one for dark tones, or choose a dominant colour to give the mood of the drawing plus two secondary colours.

COLOUR PENCILS
Colour pencils can create hatching and line to describe shapes and forms through lines, hatching, scribble, dots and so on. Start with a dominant colour to create the main shapes, and pick out other colours to use against it. Lightly draw in the outlines first, and then add colour within them. However, don't just colour in the different shapes up to an outline. Use colour pencils to make marks and create texture.

One of the difficulties with pencils is that they are all the same strength of colour, and you need to leave areas of white paper to create contrast. Also, colour pencils should be used with a more positive action than ordinary pencils in order to get a good strength of colour.

FELT-TIP PENS
Felt-tip pens are available in a large range of colours and thicknesses of tip. They create a graphic, immediate effect, but can also be used with subtlety. Put in the outlines first lightly, where needed, and then add hatching to create shadow or shape. The character of the drawing is dictated by the pen, so you don't need to try to make lots of different marks with it. Rather than putting in detail, use it to create overall tonal or colour effects. Again, choose a limited colour scheme with one dominant colour.

PASTELS
Two types of pastels are available: soft and oil. Soft pastels are chalky, and are made in a wide range of

Colour pencil. The pencils were used to create areas of single colours through hatching and line rather than solid areas. Blue was used as the main drawing colour, against which lemon yellow, yellow ochre and orange were used to isolate the figures.

Felt-tip pen. A light grey line was used to outline the buildings, and for the shapes of windows and roofs. Light blue vertical hatching creates an impression of the street and shadows. Accents were added with brown and a touch of red.

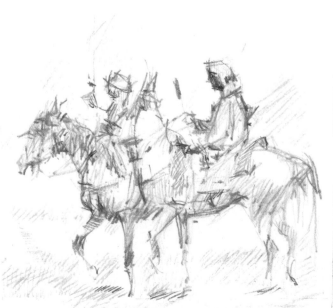

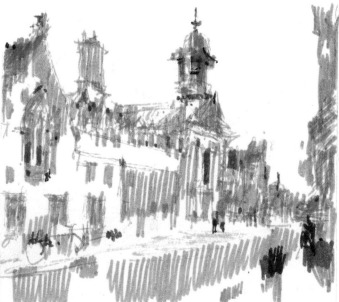

colours and tints, whereas oil pastels are slightly waxy, the colours are stronger, and they are less easy to manipulate on the paper. Whichever type you are using, the main difference between them and crayons is that you use them to create mass rather than line. From the start, block in the overall shapes, rather than outlining them. You can draw with one colour, then another, keeping each as a separate entity. First decide what colour each area will be, put it in en masse, and leave. Too much mixing and blending can make colours smudged and dirty. Limit yourself to about three colours in a drawing, and choose the colours according to your imagination, not what you see.

WAX CRAYONS

Use wax crayons for line rather than for overall blocks of colour. The colour doesn't rub, so you can use it direct and not worry about spoiling a picture while you are working on it. Wax crayons emphasize the texture of the paper, and can be used to create a variety of surface effects that are quite graphic in appearance.

USING COLOURED PAPERS

Colour pencils should be used on the lightest background possible because they do not produce very strong colours. White paper is best of all. Felt-tip pens and wax crayons are also best on lighter-coloured paper because stronger colours kill the subtle effects that they create.

Because pastels have a greater strength of colour they can be used on a full range of coloured papers. If you are using pastels on a light paper, use the paper itself for the light tones; if a mid-toned paper, use the paper for the mid-tones; if you are using a dark paper, use the paper for the dark tones. This has a unifying effect on the drawing.

With any of these materials, if you want to create a vibrant effect, choose a paper colour that contrasts with the dominant colour you are using for the drawing. If you want to create a harmonious effect, choose a paper colour close to the dominant colour in the drawing.

Coloured papers are available in a range of textures, so you need to bear in mind the effect of the surface, as well as the colour, on your materials.

Oil pastel. Two main colours were used in roughly equal quantities: ochre in the sky, outlining the shape of the church, and green to bring the eye down to the foreground. The building stands out because it was left as white paper.

Wax crayon. A very simple, graphic effect has been created by using horizontal strokes of light brown across most of the sketch, while the shape of the building was built up with vertical strokes in a dominant purple, accents and black.

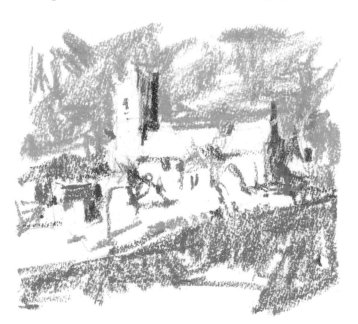

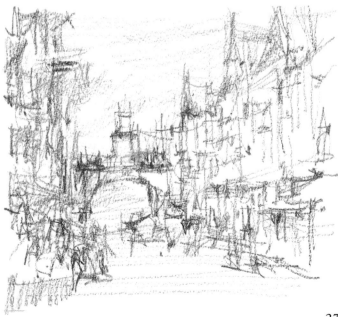

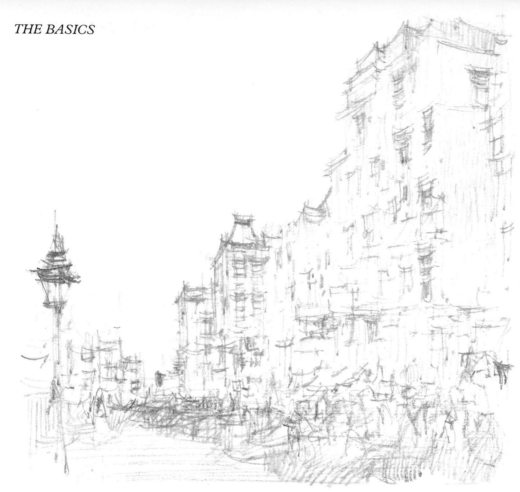

Colour pencils on cartridge paper. Colour was used to create the impression of light and shadow on the buildings, with orange describing sunlight and blue/green the shadows. Crosshatching was used in the foreground to create a base for the image. The sky was deliberately left plain to balance the areas of colour.

Felt-tip pen on white paper. Five shades of blue from light to dark were used, which creates a strong tonal effect. Put down in solid areas, felt-tip pen is too strong. It is much more effective when used in a textural way, such as with hatching. The different blocks of parallel hatching can be used to describe the different elements in the picture.

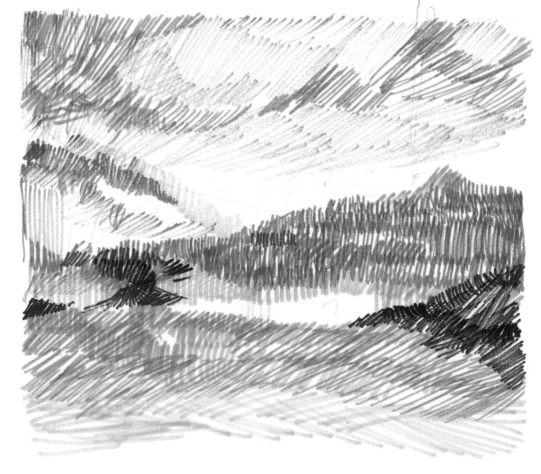

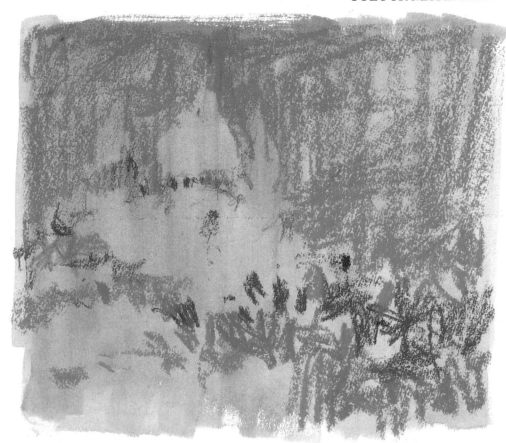

Soft and wax pastels on a beige background. The background was lightly washed on using gouache. Colour in the drawing was used to create a pattern rather than in a realistic way. Pink was used in the sky to outline the general shapes of the buildings. Orange was applied with vigorous strokes in the foreground to provide a contrast with the flat use of pastel in the sky. Pink was also used in the foreground, to tie in with the sky, and touches of blue were added to create accents.

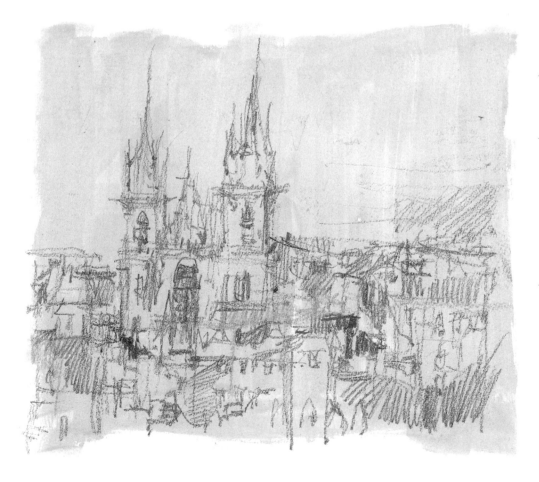

Wax crayons on a light beige background put in with gouache. The subject was treated in a very simple way, with the buildings being described just as overall shapes. A few details were sketched in, and a few areas of shadow were hatched in to give a sense of solidity. Brown was used for the main drawing, with touches of pink to provide accents. The subject was deliberately placed in the bottom half of the sketch to create a balance against the plainness of the sky.

WATERCOLOUR

Watercolour is transparent, and works through the selective use of washes applied to white paper. You need to work from light to dark because you cannot paint light colours over darker ones, and it is best to work on stretched paper (page 36).

Decide on the colour for each area of the drawing, and mix up plenty of each in advance. Then put down the colours boldly, working as quickly as possible without worrying about neatness or detail. Use thin washes and a large brush. Where you want darks, get them through your choice of colour, not through the strength of the paint. If you use a heavy paper, you can wash out areas with a small sponge and clean water and start again if necessary.

GOUACHE

Gouache is water-based, and can be used either as a thin wash or as thick paint. It is quick drying, but can be lifted off with a wet brush if you want to make changes. Being opaque, it doesn't have the translucency of watercolour, but it is easier to use because you can re-draw over what you've done, and you can apply lighter colours on top of darker ones. It can be used on board, paper or cardboard, but you should stretch paper first (page 36). Gouache can be used on smooth or textured paper, and it is worth experimenting with both to find out what effects can be created. Interesting scumbled and layered areas can be created with textured paper.

ACRYLIC

Acrylic paint is water-based, and dries quickly, although colours dry slightly lighter. It can be used on paper, board or canvas, and can either be applied as thin washes or used thickly like oil paint. Acrylics dry permanently, so a second wash will not disturb the original one, unlike watercolour or gouache, where a second wash will partly lift off the original wash and mix with it, thereby degrading the colours. This allows acrylics to be used to build up layers of washes if wanted.

Always wash brushes after each application of colour, because acrylic paint can ruin brushes as it dries so quickly.

Right, the paint was applied directly with the brush using a limited number of colours and letting the watercolour create the effect of mist on the water. Often these accidental effects can be as interesting as those you try to achieve deliberately. One wash was used to create the overall shape. Blue was added and allowed to spread into the foreground. On the right-hand side, warmer colour was applied over the dry wash to give the building hard edges.

Far right, a more finished drawing in which the shape of the horse was applied over a dry wash. When this was dry, accents of brown and black were applied to give more definition.

Right, an overall background wash was applied, and the grey and red shapes were added over the top when this was dry. The grey was slightly watery so it has mixed a little with the wash underneath. The red and green were applied quite dry with dragged brushstrokes to pick up the texture of the paper and let some of the original wash show through.

Far right, a blue background wash was applied, and then the outlines of the features were added. Colour was scumbled over the foreground and roof, and a second wash was applied over the sky.

Right, a background wash was applied in varying strengths and allowed to dry. The subject was then quickly sketched in, utilizing the texture of the paper.

Far right, a more detailed and finished study in which the sky, cliffs and sea were blocked in over a grey/green background. Brushstrokes emphasize the surface of the sea and the boat has been put in with white impasto.

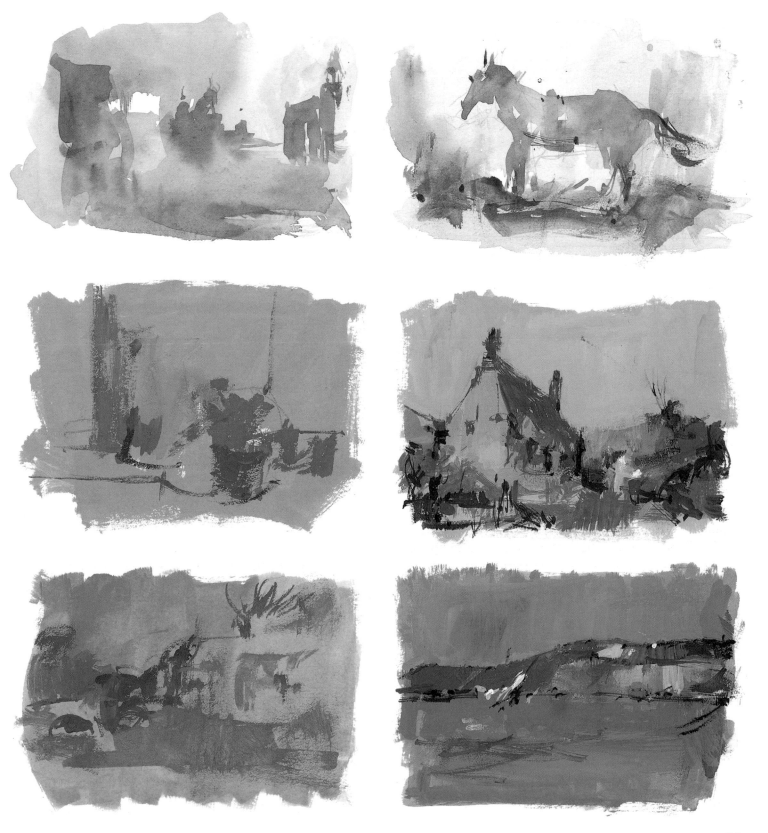

Practice

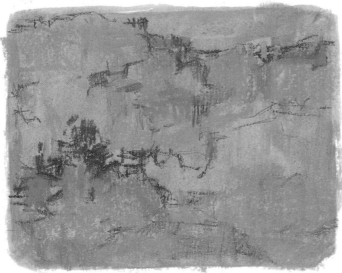

Try a pastel drawing on a coloured background put on with gouache. Choose a simple landscape and break it down into the main shapes. Use one colour to outline the main shapes, and then block them in using the main colour. Add touches of one to two contrasting colours to break up the main colour and create accents of interest.

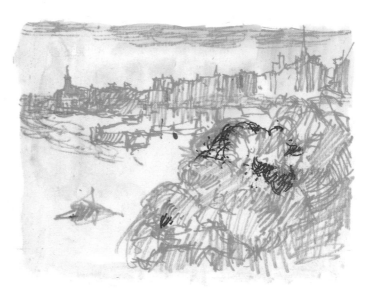

Felt-tip pen. Choose buildings and trees for this drawing, and use a light wash background. Keep to three colours, the dominant colour and two others that provide a contrast, and concentrate on using line and crosshatching to create the shapes and tones in the subject. Aim to create a balance between busy and empty areas of the drawing.

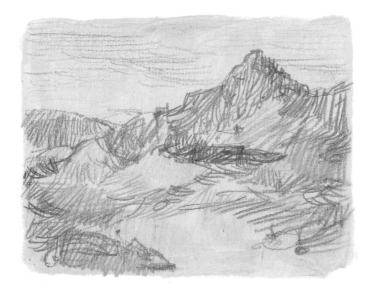

Colour pencil. An open landscape with hills is a good subject for colour pencils. Again work on a coloured background. Outline the main shapes very lightly to start with, and then build up the drawing with blocks of hatching, using different colours to create the image. Vary the direction of the hatching to convey different planes.

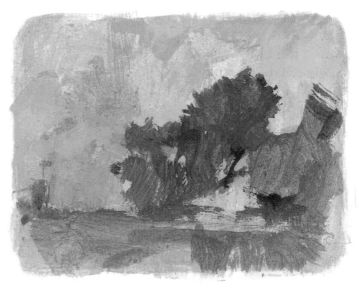

Acrylics. Choose a landscape with strong, simple shapes. First put down a mid-toned wash over the whole area, and let this provide the mid tones in the drawing. Sketch in the main shapes with a darker colour. When dry, use a light colour for the sky and to add highlights against the dark areas, but keep it to a minimum.

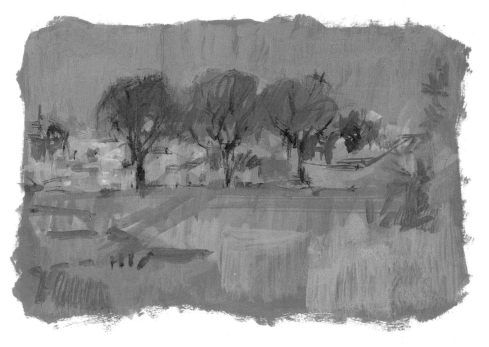

Right, gouache. Put down an overall background wash, and sketch in the main features of the drawing lightly with pencil. Then block in the main areas. Use three or four colours and try to work quickly, drawing with the brush and using directional brushstrokes.

Below, watercolour. Choose a landscape or beach scene. Draw in the skyline and main shapes lightly, mapping out the areas for the washes and planning where to leave areas of white paper. Use a wet wash in the sky, dampening areas of paper and letting the wash run into them, but don't go below the horizon. When dry, add the mid-tones. Then run a wash across the foreground in one brushstroke.

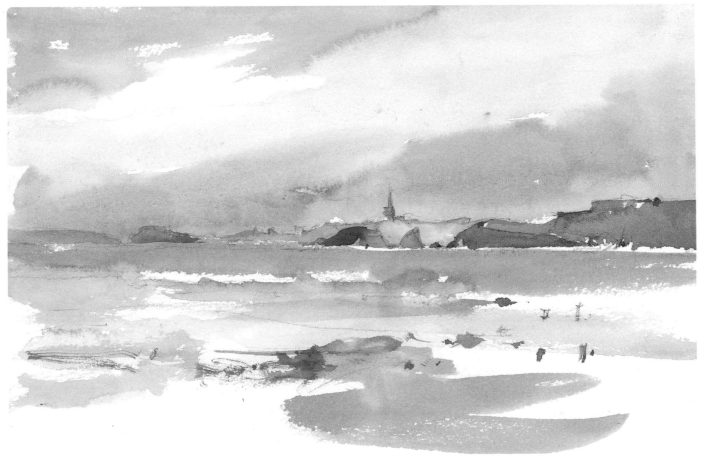

Techniques

MIXED MEDIA

It is possible to enhance the effects of one medium by using it in combination with another. For example, you might be using watercolour because you like its translucent effect, but this can be emphasized by the addition of a little drawing work in pencil or crayon. Alternatively, the delicacy of pencil can be highlighted by the addition of a wash. Pen and ink used in combination with watercolour, on the other hand, provides a sharp, almost brutal, contrast. When you are deciding which materials to combine, try to think in terms of compatibility or contrast and what will suit the subject.

The essence of mixed media is experimentation. You only have a limited amount of control over what happens, so don't try to use the materials in a controlled way. Instead, allow random effects to occur and let the paper contribute to the effect as much as possible.

When using pencil and wash, you can either do the pencil drawing first and apply the wash around and over the pencil to describe the shape of the subject, or you can apply the wash first to map out areas of colour and draw over it.

The addition of oil pastel over gouache paint creates interesting effects. The oil pastel lies on the surface of the paint, rather than sinking into the paper, so the colours remain very bright against the paint. This means that oil pastel can be applied over dark colours without being degraded by the paint underneath, whereas an additional layer of paint would mix with the previous layer and become dirty.

Water-resist techniques are fun to try. Wax crayon or oil pastel is applied first, and a watercolour or gouache wash is laid on over the top. The wash won't take over the waxy areas, and some lovely random effects can be achieved.

Try small-scale sketches to start with using these techniques. It is best to work on cartridge paper while you get to know them. Then move on to textured and coloured papers and find out what additional effects they can create. Roughly plot out the chosen subject in pencil, but be ready to respond to any effects that happen.

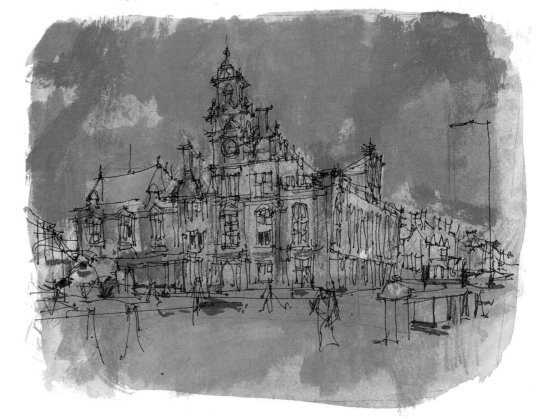

A light pink wash was applied to bring out the texture of the watercolour paper. The blue-grey sky was then applied with quite thick gouache paint to kill the texture in the sky. The building was drawn in with a fine felt-tip pen. Texture on the building was emphasized with conté pencil, which also creates an impression of solidity and bulk.

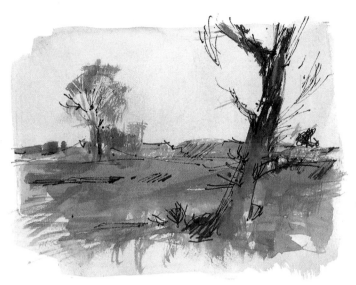

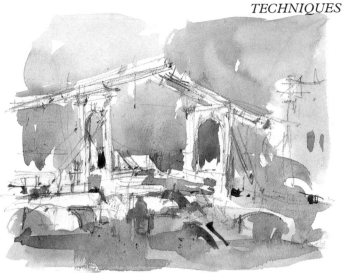

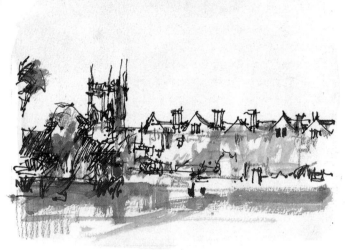

Above, first a watercolour wash was applied all over. Gouache was used in the foreground and very dry on the left-hand tree and right-hand tree trunk; pen and ink were used to draw around the branches of the tree; and pink oil pastel was applied for the distant fields.

Above right, the main shapes of the bridge were drawn in pencil, and a watercolour wash was applied round the bridge to accentuate its shape. A second, darker wash was applied under the bridge when the first was dry.

Right, a thin overall gouache wash was applied first. Gouache was scumbled on in the foreground; colour pencil was used round the buildings; and pen and ink were applied last for the main drawing.

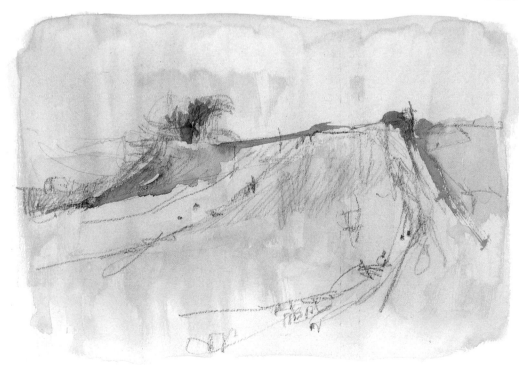

Left, a grey watercolour wash was applied quite dry. Pencil lines were drawn on over the wash to create the main shapes in the landscape. A darker grey wash was applied at an angle, and blue crayon was added in places to create accents of colour.

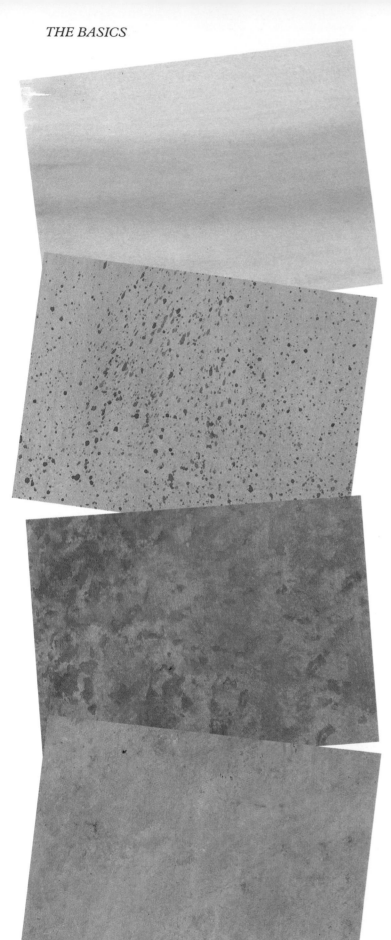

PREPARED BACKGROUNDS
It is worth preparing coloured and textured grounds in batches so that you have always got something ready to work on. Prepared backgrounds can themselves provide inspiration for pieces of work.

STRETCHING PAPER
Paper that is going to be used with water-based materials needs to be stretched first to prevent it cockling when it is wet. This consists of wetting the paper, taping it down and letting it dry so it can't stretch any more when it becomes wet from the application of washes.

   Cut a sheet of paper to the size you want. Either submerge it in a bowl of water, or hold it under the tap, making sure that the paper is thoroughly soaked – this will take only a few seconds. Place the paper on a drawing board. Tear off four strips of gummed tape – one for each side of the paper – and wet the gummed side. Tape down the top edge of the paper, smooth out the paper against the board, and tape down the bottom edge. Then tape down the two side edges. Sponge off the surplus water and let the paper dry naturally. Once the paper is dry, you can give yourself a base to work on by adding a simple wash or a textured background.

LAYING A SIMPLE WASH
Mix more of the colour you are using than you think you will need. Dampen the surface of the paper

Top left, vignette; left, stipple; below left, sponge; below, cloth.

Top right, pen and wash have been lightly applied over a vignette background – mainly over the middle band of stronger colour which gives form to the boats.

Right, a blue-grey wash has been applied to the sky, leaving the stipple to suggest texture in the foreground.

Below right, blue gouache has been applied to the sky, and loose crayon and gouache create the impression of trees in the foreground. The textured background unifies the drawing.

Below, blue has been applied to the background around the outlines of the figure, and the texture creates atmosphere.

lightly, and tilt the drawing board slightly. Using a
large brush, load it with colour and apply the wash
across the top of the paper in one continuous stroke.
Work horizontally down the paper in this way,
picking up the bottom edge of the wash with each
new application.

TEXTURED BACKGROUNDS

Textured backgrounds can create atmosphere and
unity in a drawing, and suggest textural effects.

A vignette effect – where one colour diffuses into
another – can be created by damping the paper and
running a lighter colour half-way down it. Use
another brush and a stronger colour and lay it on
across the middle of the paper. Then go back to the
original wash and brush for the rest of the paper.
The stronger colour will diffuse into the original
colour on either side.

Stipple can be created by laying a wash all over
the paper and letting it dry. Then load a brush with
another colour and tap the brush gently as you move
it across the area you want to cover.

Sponging can create an interesting background to
work on. After laying an initial wash and letting it
dry, load a sponge with colour and squeeze it out
again so that it is semi-dry. Then press it on to the
paper. Keep applying colour until you have the
strength you require. You can add specks of a
slightly stronger colour if you want. A screwed-up
cloth can be used to create texture in the same way.

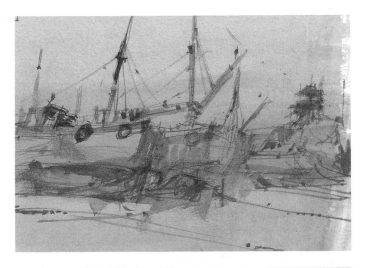

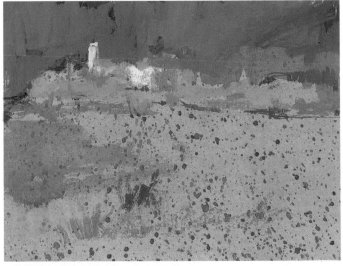

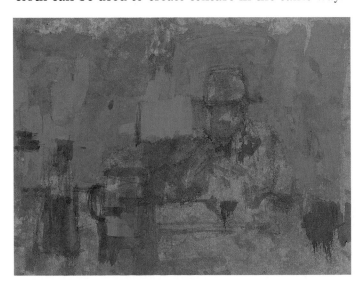

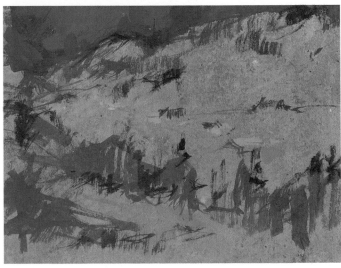

MEASURING

One of the basic skills in drawing is the use of a pencil to measure the relative size and proportions of your subject. The usual way of doing this is to use the pencil held at arm's length. Hold it upright in line with the section of the subject you are measuring and align the tip of the pencil with the top of the section you are measuring. Mark where the bottom is on the pencil with your thumb. As long as you stand in exactly the same position each time you measure, and hold the pencil at a constant distance from your eye; the measurements will always be constant.

It is best to select a section of the subject to use as your measuring unit, and to relate all other parts of the subject and its surroundings to this. If you are drawing a figure, the top of the head to the chin is a good unit to use as it will not vary. Or you could use something in the background that you are going to include in the drawing. Measure your chosen unit with a pencil, and then move the pencil down the subject – keeping your thumb in place – to see how many times your measuring unit divides into the height of the subject. Transfer these proportions to your paper. Once you have established the vertical proportions you can then take the horizontal

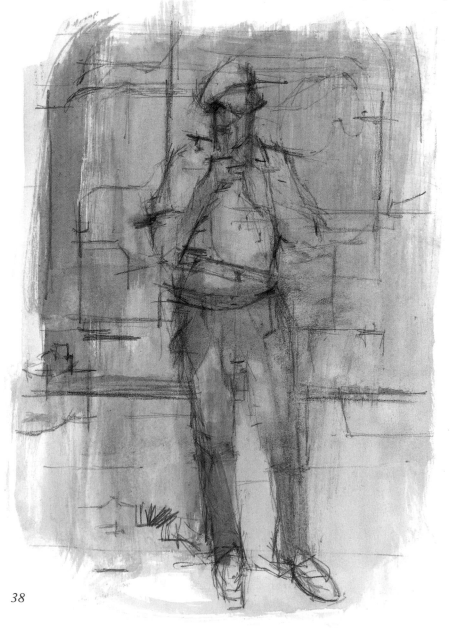

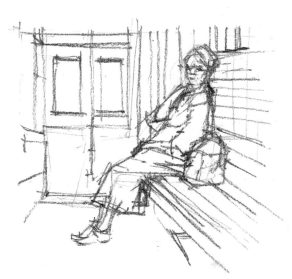

Above, the use of vertical and diagonal lines place the figure in a space. The impression of space in front of the figure is created by linear perspective (page 102).

Left, the figure is standing in front of a door, which provides horizontal and vertical lines against which the figure can be assessed. The vertical lines give the angle of the right arm and the legs. Horizontal lines give the angle of the brow, the slant of the shoulders, and the relative positions of the elbows and of the knees.

measurements using the same unit of measurement.

Take these measurements before you start a drawing and mark off the positions of different parts of the subject on the paper so that you know where things should be in relation to each other before you begin. With time and practice, you may not need to measure before you start, but even then it is a good way to check any drawing as you go along.

ESTABLISHING ANGLES
You can establish the angles within the subject that you are drawing by assessing them against upright or horizontal lines within or around the subject. Things like windows and doors, or buildings if you are outside, provide a natural grid against which you can judge the angles within the subject. Real or

imagined vertical and horizontal lines will also help you see which parts of the subject are directly below others – something that is easy to get wrong when you are judging just by eye, especially when drawing a figure. You can also hold up a pencil to check this.

If you plot the proportions and relative positions of different parts of your subject using these techniques, you will find that the drawing – whether of a figure, still life, building or landscape – takes shape quite naturally.

Once you have decided on the unit of measurement within your subject, you can use it to measure diagonal lines as well as horizontal and vertical ones. Here, the depth of the head was used to establish the correct position of the subject's right hand by dividing it into the line formed from the cheek down the arm to the hand, and seeing where this met an imagined perpendicular dropped from the line of the door.

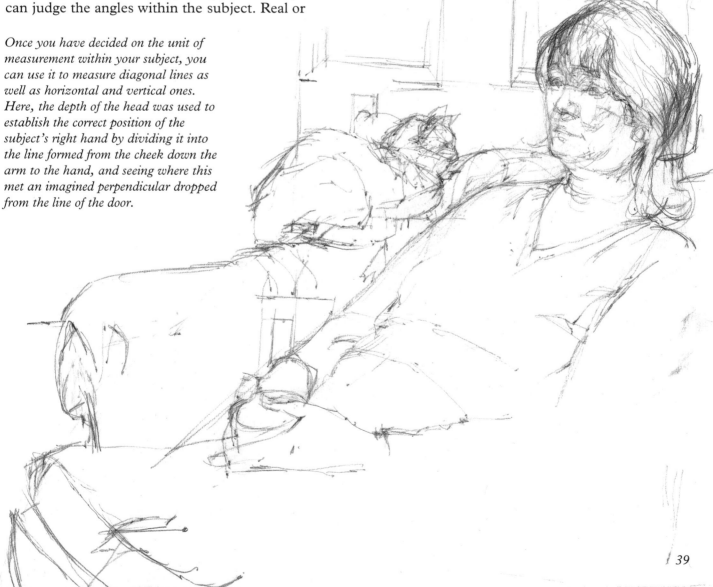

COLLECTING REFERENCES

One of the pleasures of visiting new places lies in bringing back sketches and objects associated with the trip, from which you can make more finished studies and drawings. And by sketching on the spot, it is possible to create a liveliness and sense of atmosphere that is not the case with more considered drawings.

Once away from the subject, you will probably find that you need more information than you have collected. Remember to make notes on colours, tones, times of day, weather conditions, the direction of the light, types of trees or vegetation, names or numbers on boats and writing on signs, as such details will all help you to recreate the atmosphere of the place. Collect things like pebbles, shells, flowers, grasses, driftwood, and any other small objects that have an interesting colour or texture or are characteristic of the place.

Try to make sure that you have included every object and shape in your sketches, even if it is just with a single line. You can always sketch details separately. You can also take photographs, but if you are going to work from these, use several not just one, so that you are not merely copying from them. Photographs are best used as an aide memoire rather than for working from directly.

When you return home, some of the things that you were looking at and drawing will come back into your memory, so although you may be working from images in your sketchbook and objects, you will find that you have the freedom to alter and play around with them creating new compositions.

Quick, loose watercolour sketches provide a guide to composition. Pencil notes can be added on time of day, colours, and direction of the light. Pencil sketches provide additional information that cannot be included in a watercolour sketch.

More detailed, finished studies made at home from objects – pebbles, shells, small fir cones, bits of plants and a piece of rusting metal – brought back from a trip to the beach. Pencil and wash, with some splatter, have been used effectively to convey their varying forms and textures.

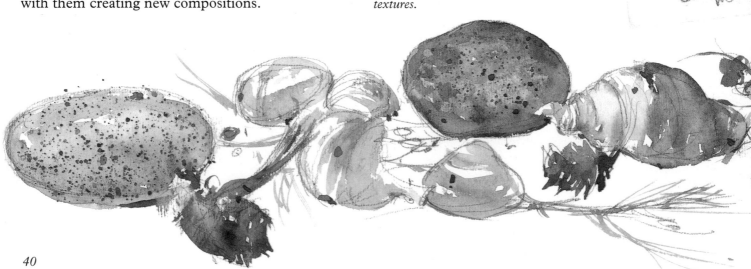

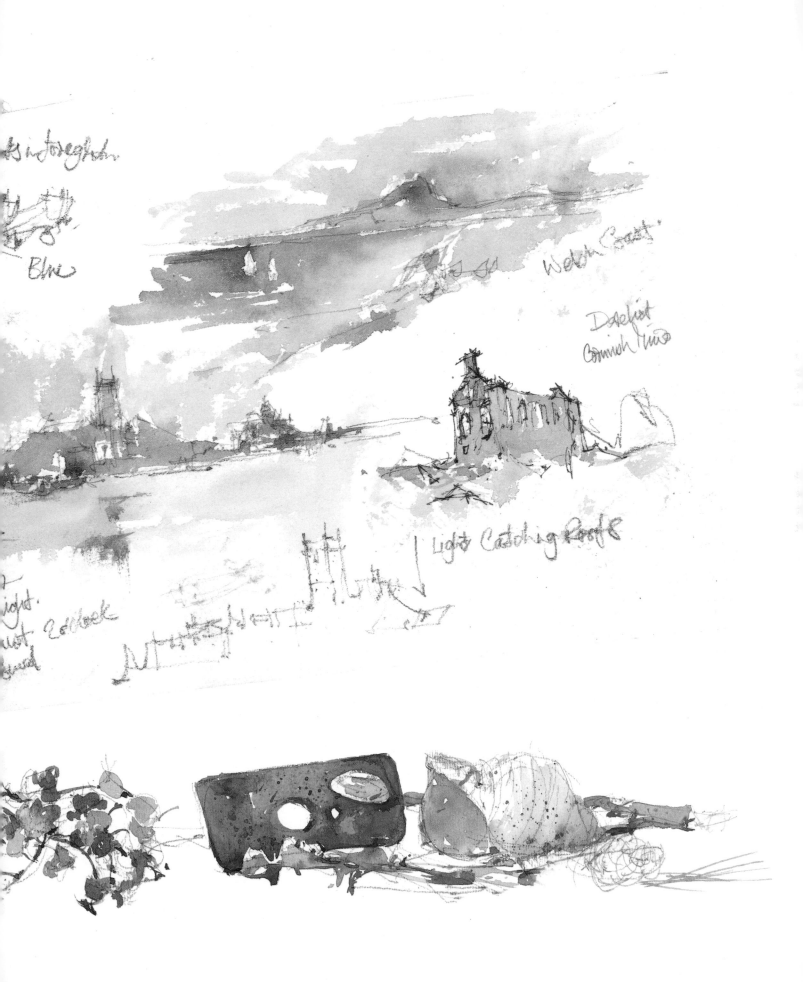

Welsh Coast

Darkest Cornish Mine

light Catching Roofs

Blue

Tonal Values

Tonal values represent the range of tones from light to dark in any subject and any drawing. Tone can be used to give a sense of form and space, or to enhance the effect of a picture and create atmosphere. You need to decide which approach you are going to take before you start, because using tone for pictorial effect involves flattening the image and giving it a more abstract quality. Everybody sees tones slightly differently, but it is the way in which you use them in your work that is critical.

SEEING TONE
When looking at a subject, don't look at tones in isolation. They must always be assessed one against another in different parts of the subject. Compare adjacent tones, and compare tones in the foreground against those in the distance.

It is easy to be fooled by the effects of distance because most people are more sensitive to colour than tone, and are misled into thinking that something is a darker tone than it really is because of its colour. It is essential, therefore, to keep comparing tones in the foreground against those in the distance, and vice versa. Don't assume that something which is white or very light-coloured is automatically light in tone. Compare it with other light areas in the subject, because it may be darker than you at first thought.

Objects are also affected by reflected light from the objects around them, as well as by light from the main light source, and you need to look for the effects that this has on your subject, particularly on the side facing away from the light source. This is particularly important if you want to create an impression of three-dimensional forms in your drawing.

When you are drawing, do not assume that the first tone you put down is correct, compared to what you have seen. The tonal values of different areas of your drawing will alter in relation to each other when you put other tones down beside them. You need to keep evaluating tones in different parts of a drawing as you go along and make adjustments in order to keep the balance right.

The following exercise will help you see the way in which a tone alters in relation to the tone that is laid down next to it. It is best done with gouache paint. Mix white and black to make a mid-grey and divide this into four batches. Mix a touch of red into one batch, a touch of yellow into the second, a touch of blue into the third and a touch of black into the last. On a sheet of paper paint a square of each tint of grey. Take a piece of white card and a piece of black card and cut a hole in the middle, smaller than your painted squares. Lay first the white card and then the black card over each grey square in turn and see how the tone of each square alters against the white and black. This changing of tones in relation to each other occurs all the time when

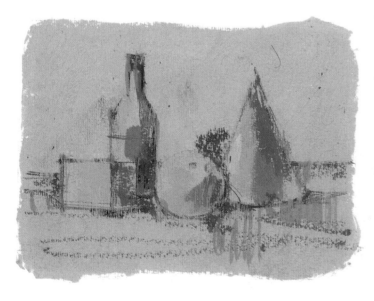

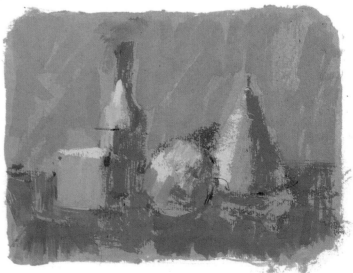

you are drawing and painting, and it is important to be able to see it happening so that you can make adjustments.

DESCRIBING FORM

The interplay of light, dark and mid tones can be used in a drawing to give a three-dimensional quality to objects. Light creates the forms and shapes of objects through light and shadow, because it strikes some surfaces and not others. Therefore when using tone to create form, you should be using the tonal range to describe the way light is falling on the subject. It is not just a matter of copying areas of light and dark.

Make a mental note of the direction of the light, and decide which planes are receiving light and which are in shadow. To simplify a subject, you can break the tones down into three – light, mid and dark – and describe the subject in these three tones. Then change the direction of the light on the same set-up and see how forms and shadows, and the whole character of the subject, changes. You can then progress to using five and then seven tones to describe a subject.

To make a curved surface look as if it is turning away from you, make changes in tone as gradual as possible – the greater the number of steps from a light to mid tone or mid to dark, the more gradually the surface will turn away. If you want to describe a sharp edge, such as the edge made by two sides of a cube, a sharper contrast of light against dark will give the sudden change in direction of the surface.

You can do a simple exercise to see the way in which different tones placed next to each other create different modelling effects. Mix up four greys from light to dark. On a piece of paper or card, paint a strip of each and cut them out. Try arranging the strips in a row in different combinations – first light to dark, then medium/light/dark/medium. The first arrangement will give an impression of gradual modelling, whereas the light-dark juxtaposition in the second arrangement will suggest an edge.

DO'S AND DON'TS

Do assess tones against one another in different parts of the subject.

Do notice the way in which tones in your drawing alter as you put down other tones next to them.

Do look for the effects of reflected light within the subject.

Do look for the way that light reveals the forms in your subject.

Don't make contrasts too strong when you want to describe a smoothly curving surface.

Don't just copy areas of light and dark.

These studies were made in gouache and oil pastel. Light was coming from the left, striking the sides of the objects facing that way; the other sides were in shadow. In the far left picture, a limited range of tones has been used, from light to mid grey, with dark accents to emphasize the shapes of the objects. Centre, the background is darker, bringing into play the light catching the objects from the left, which gives more modelling.

Near left, the background is darker still, and a full range of tones has been used from light to dark. As a result, the objects are more rounded and three-dimensional. The greater the range of tones used, the stronger the modelling effect and the more the individual objects are emphasized.

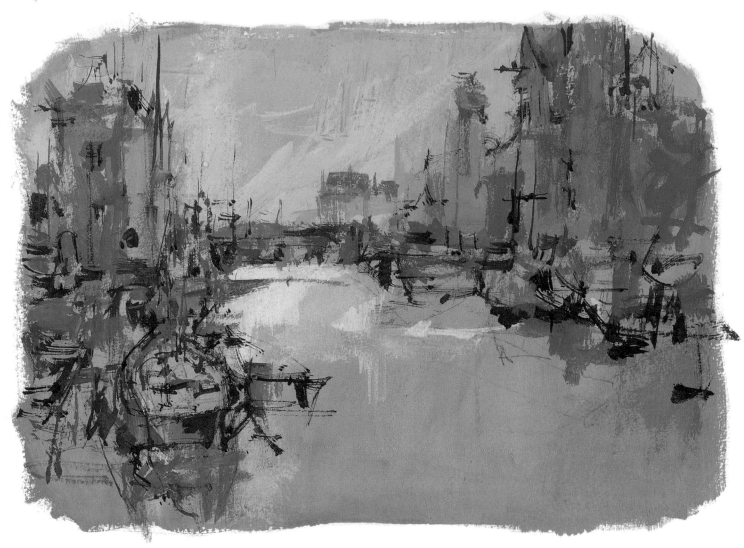

TONE AND SPACE

A basic guideline in the use of tone to create the impression of space and distance is that extreme light and dark tones and strong tonal contrasts occur in the foreground, and the degree of contrast decreases with distance. This effect is known as aerial perspective, and creative use of this can give an impression of space in a drawing.

Another way of creating the impression of space is to observe where a tone in the foreground matches one in the background. A darker tone separating the two, creating an alternation between light and dark, can also give an impression of distance.

Having said this, there are times when you can find stronger tones and more contrast in the mid or far distance than in the foreground. Interesting effects can be achieved by imitating this in a drawing.

This was done in acrylic and the range of tones was restricted to four. Stronger tonal contrasts have been used in the mid-distance than in the foreground. A sense of space is achieved through the alternation of tones that are not too far apart in value in the foreground, leading back to the bridge. The strong contrast between the dark bridge and the light area on the water immediately in front of it also draws the eye through the scene to that point.

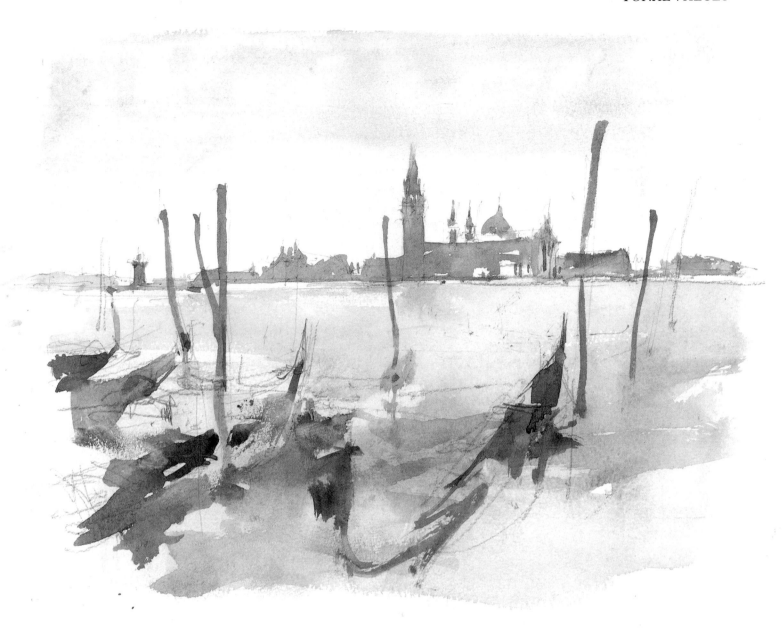

A light wash was applied all over for the sky and water. Mid tones were used for the buildings in the background. Dark tones were used in the foreground to create a strong contrast with the light wash, against which the scene recedes into the distance. The sky too decreases in intensity towards the horizon, which also contributes to the feeling of depth in the scene. Drawings like this, where the tones are massed together to form simple shapes, can be more atmospheric than ones where lots of detail are included.

TONE AND COLOUR

When working in colour, it is possible to achieve tonal effects by 'greying' the colours you are using rather than by making them lighter or darker. This can be done by adding small amounts of black and white, or by adding a colour's complementary. The complementary pairs are blue/orange, red/green and yellow/violet. A bright colour will advance against a greyer one, and this can be used to describe forms and the spaces between them. By keeping all colours to approximately the same tone, and describing form through the varying greyness of the colours, you can put everything – both objects and the spaces between them – on the same visual plane, thereby giving the drawing an overall surface unity.

TONAL QUALITY

Tone can be used in other ways than for creating realistic modelling and an impression of space. It can be used to create atmosphere, and can transform an ordinary subject – whether a figure, still life or landscape – into something rather beautiful, even to the extent where a drawing is appreciated for its tonal quality rather than for its subject.

If you are using tone for its tonal quality rather than for modelling, you need to see and treat tones as abstract shapes, and this approach is most successful if you work in a limited range of tones. When working in this way, concentrate on the tonal pattern you want to achieve in the drawing rather than matching tones that you see in the subject. If you are working in colour, see what effects you can get by working with just two colours, together with the intermediary greys you get from mixing them, and adding white to create a limited range of tones.

One way of working with limited tones that produces very effective results is to transcribe a subject into a high-key or low-key range of tones. A high-key drawing is one in light to mid tones, with the darkest tone in the drawing being in the middle of the range, and one or two dark accents for contrast. A low-key drawing is done in mid to dark tones, with one or two light accents. This has the effect of condensing the range of tones into a narrow band, and can be used to create very subtle images.

TONE AND COMPOSITION

Whichever approach to tone you take, you need to be aware of the pattern that will be created by tonal areas within your drawing. You also need to remember that strong tonal contrasts draw the eye, so use them to focus the viewer's attention where you want it. Plan to keep the lighter and darker areas away from the edges of the picture area because a strong tonal effect at the edge can lead the eye out of the picture. Also keep them away from the centre so that they don't draw attention away from the main interest.

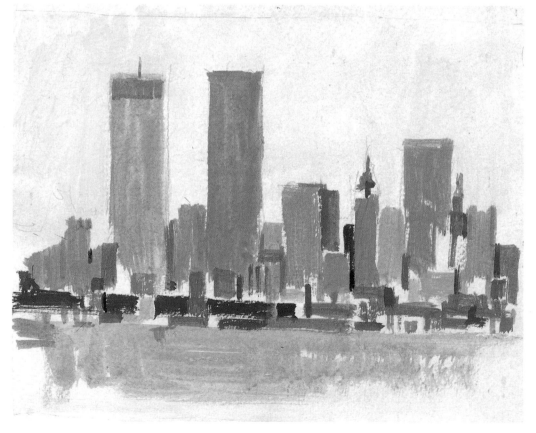

Left, pattern has been created in this cityscape through blocks of different colours set against each other. The drawing works because the tones have been kept within a limited range from medium light to medium dark, with small blocks providing dark accents. The white paper showing around the blocks is essential, because if the tones were butted up, they would merge and kill each other.

Right, this was done using two tones plus the white of the paper. The mid-toned chalk was used for all tones except the lightest and darkest. The dark tone was used sparingly to emphasize the forms of the objects rather than to put in the shadows that were evident.

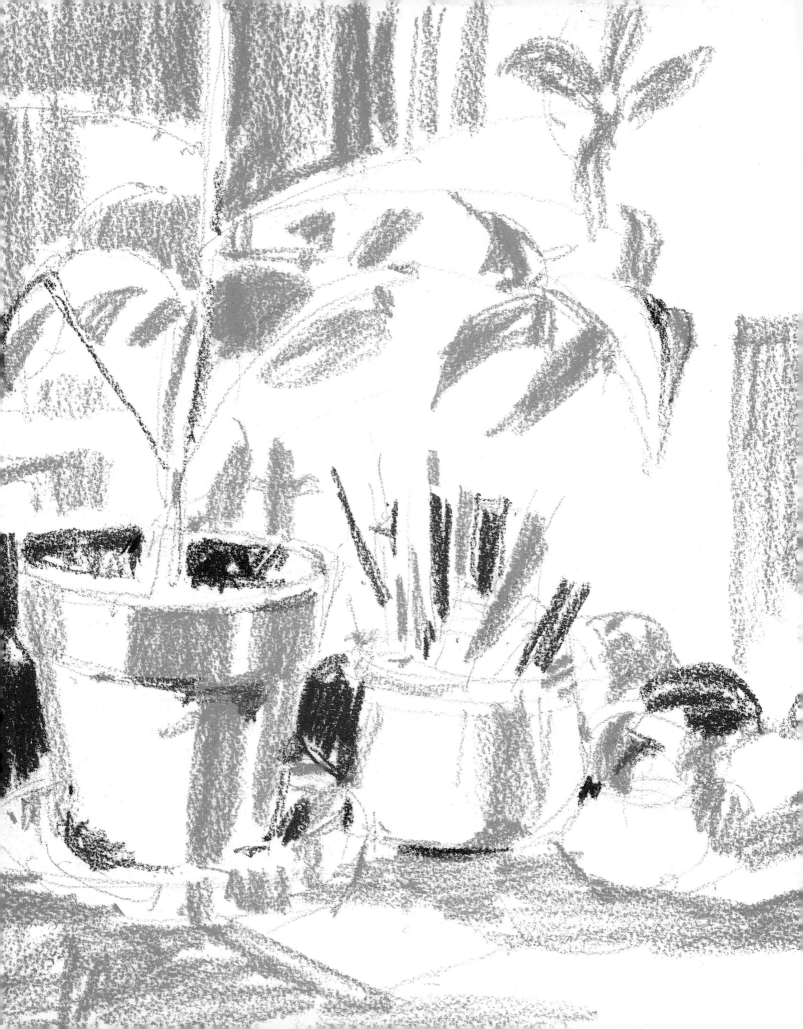

Practice

Take simple subjects and try different approaches to using tone. First try using hatching to create modelling, then, still working in monochrome, draw a subject by putting in large blocks of tone – with just three or five tones – and use the tones to create the shapes and forms of the objects regardless of whether you see the tones in the subject or not.

When simplifying a subject into three or five tones, see areas of tone as abstract shapes, and leave areas of the drawing unstated so that the eye can complete it. Then try working in colour, using colours in a close tonal range and greying them to describe forms and space. Finally, using a limited range of colours and tones, try to create atmospheric effects without worrying about capturing the three-dimensional nature of the things you are drawing. Gouache is a good medium for the exercises incorporating colour, because you can make corrections over the top of what you have done already until you get a drawing that satisfies you.

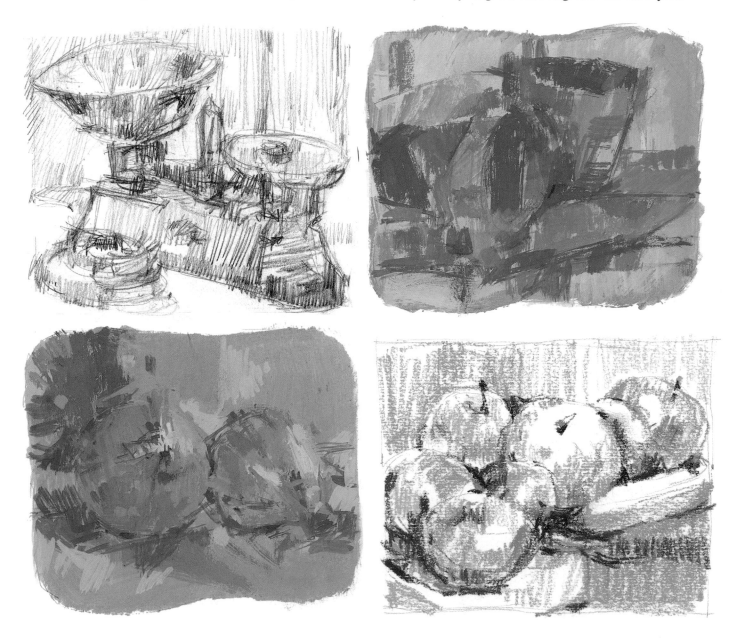

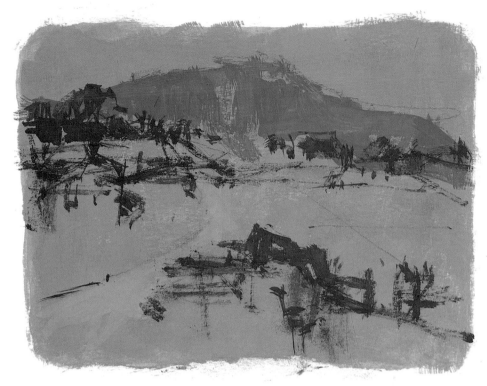

Left, make a study of a scene using just two colours and three tones. Put down a mid-toned background first, so that you have something to measure your light and dark tones against. Mix the three tones before you start – here the light tone is a beige-grey, the mid tone a medium brown and the dark tone a dark brown. Use the three tones against each other to create a sense of distance in the picture.

Below, use two colours again, but mix a bigger range of tones – say, seven – and use them to create a sense of atmosphere by treating areas of tone as flat, abstract shapes. By working around the subject with darker and lighter tones it is possible to describe the shape of the subject at the same time.

Far left, top, make a pencil study of a simple object, using line to build up areas of tone.

Left, top, try translating tone into colour. Mix up five colours in similar tones, and use them to describe the shape and form of an object.

Far left, this was done in acrylics. Set up a simple still life lit from one direction, and try to capture the shapes of the objects using a limited range of tones to describe them.

Left, choose a selection of objects and, ignoring their colours, draw the shapes with three tones – here two were used plus the white of the paper. Treat all the objects as being the same tone, and put in the dark tone to emphasize forms rather than to indicate the darker local colours.

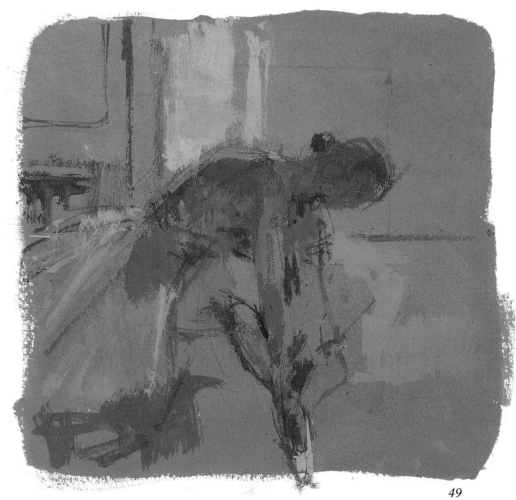

Composition

Composition is the process of arranging and placing the different elements of a picture within the frame. It is the basis of any drawing or painting, whatever medium you are working in. There are guidelines that you can follow, which will help you compose pictures in a pleasing way, but you should not treat them as unbreakable rules.

Pictures can be organized according to the rule of thirds. Mentally divide the picture area into thirds both horizontally and vertically. Strong horizontal and vertical elements in the drawing can coincide with these lines. The points where these lines intersect are good places to locate the main interest.

A triangular arrangement has been used by many artists, especially in the composition of figure studies. The triangle should be implied: locate points of interest or accents at its three corners, and suggest the sides through linear elements or the edges of shapes. A triangle standing on its base gives a picture a feeling of stability, whereas an inverted triangle creates an insecure feeling.

The composition of a picture can be based on a circle, which should be off centre and not too obvious or deliberate. It should be suggested through different elements within the picture, and is more interesting if it is not complete. A circular composition can create a sense of movement because it encourages the eye to travel around the picture.

A picture can be arranged on the diagonal within the frame, but the slope of the diagonal shouldn't take the eye out of the picture. You need to have a counterbalance in the bottom part of the picture, or counterbalancing lines working against the main direction of the composition, or an important element along the diagonal to send the eye back into the picture. Diagonals can be used to create an impression of deep space.

It is a good idea to do a small sketch, or series of sketches, to plan the composition before starting a

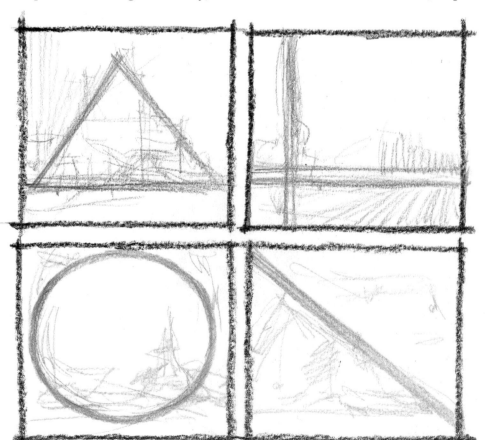

Four basic compositional shapes
Top far left, a triangular arrangement will always keep the subject within the frame of the drawing. The symmetry of the triangle can be varied.

Top left, the rule of thirds is a sound compositional guide. It can be used to the right or left of a drawing, and top or bottom.

Bottom far left, do not follow round the perimeter of a circle faithfully, break it where it seems appropriate.

Bottom left, use the diagonal with discretion. The main diagonal is best broken by subsidiary lines in the opposite direction.

drawing. Try not to place your main interest at the centre of the drawing or at the edge. And avoid having unbroken lines across or down a drawing because they can unintentionally split it into two. Look at the shapes made by different parts of the drawing, and make sure they balance each other within the frame. Also check that shapes don't unintentionally repeat each other. When a drawing is finished, it is always possible to reframe it with a mount in order to improve the composition.

SELECTION

When you are out sketching, you may sometimes find yourself presented with too big a choice of subjects or options, from which it is difficult to choose what to do. In this case, it is a good idea to use a viewfinder. Either cut a rectangle out of a piece of card, or hold up your hands to form the required shape. This will help you isolate sections of the scene and assess whether they will make a strong composition on their own. Even if you know a landscape well, a viewfinder can help you to see arrangements and relationships within it that you had not noticed before.

You can always alter or re-arrange features within a subject to improve the composition. Things can be added, left out, extended or shortened, tilted, or grouped together, in order to strengthen the picture and focus the viewer's attention where you want it.

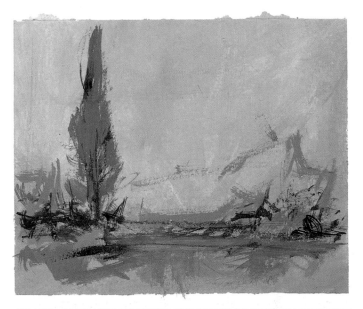

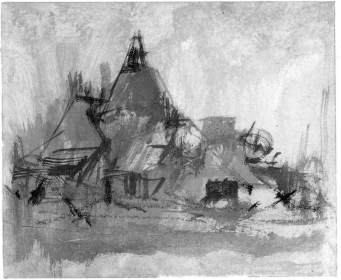

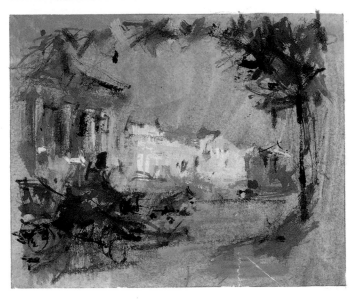

Top right, this is based on the rule of thirds. The line of the tree on the left-hand side is one-third in from the side of the picture, and the foreground fills the bottom third of the picture. This is counterbalanced by the shape on the right-hand side extending up into the sky.

Middle right, the main subject is grouped into a triangular shape, with the accents falling on the points of the triangle.

Bottom right, a circular composition is created by the trees in the top right corner, the building in the top left, the figures and shadow in the bottom left and the shadow in the bottom right. The areas of shadow forming the circle are counterbalanced by the light tones within it.

Right, when you are presented with a scene like this, you have got several options: the church and village on the left form a pleasing unit, with one cottage against another building up into an attractive pattern; on the right, the arched bridge works well against the buildings receding into the background; the boats in the foreground form interesting shapes against the buildings behind them; and the spire in the distance makes a nice shape against the sky-line. Having selected your subject, choose the format – upright or landscape – that suits it.

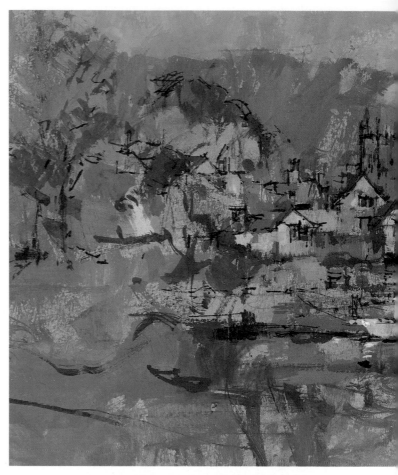

Below, because the spire is tall an upright format is best, which also allows some foreground to be included.

Below right, this format suits a detailed study of the boats and also allows some of the buildings behind to be included.

Opposite, below left, a square format frames the bridge well while providing enough space for the buildings behind.

Opposite, below right, to capture the church and its surrounding buildings, a very wide landscape format works best.

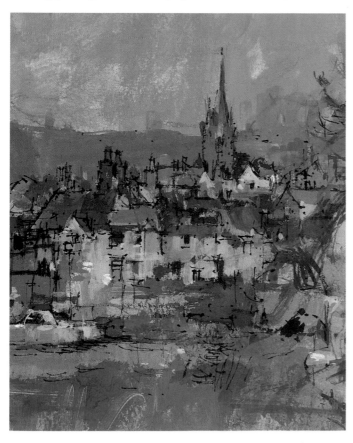

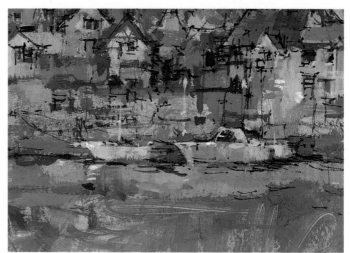

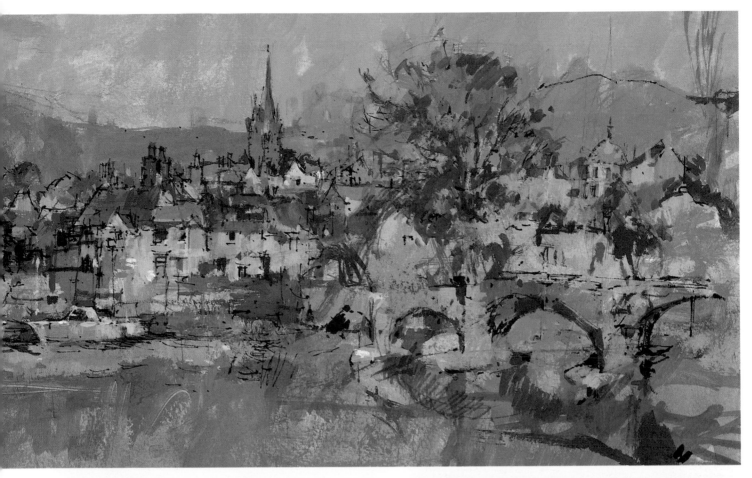

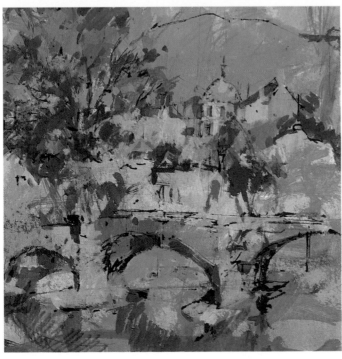

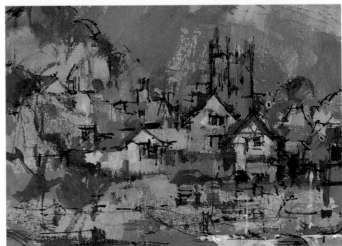

Practice

A good way to learn about composition is to study the work of great painters, and the best way to do this is to make copies, either sketching in galleries or from books or postcards at home. One of the great things about making copies is that a lot of what you discover sticks in your mind, which is why it is such a helpful way to learn. When you are making copies to study composition, have a good look at the painting before you start, and decide what you think is the basis of the composition. These studies can be done in pencil or paint. You are not trying to copy everything in the painting – concentrate on what you think are the important compositional elements. Also, work in your own style.

These studies of well-known paintings were done in gouache in a loose style.

MR AND MRS ANDREWS, *Thomas Gainsborough*
Gainsborough was not only known for his portraits, but was also an acknowledged master of landscape. In this painting he combined both attributes. The figures are arranged in a triangular shape with the vertical of the tree behind adding to the sense of stability, counterbalanced by the landscape that disappears into the distance.

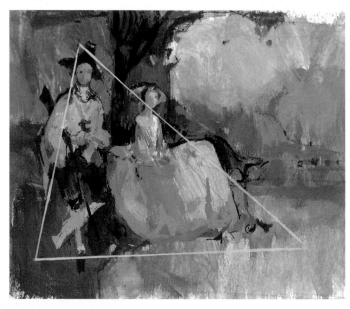

DEDHAM LOCK AND MILL, *John Constable*
Constable kept very much to the traditional rules of composition, using the rule of thirds here. However, there are subtleties in the sky and subsidiary groups of trees that prevent the picture becoming too static. Small details keep your eye moving around the scene.

THE SUPPER AT EMMAUS, *Caravaggio*
This painting contains some wonderful figure painting and a dramatic use of light within the composition. Caravaggio has used the counterchange of light against dark at the peak of the triangle to draw the eye to Christ's face. Shadows suggest the sides of the triangle, and the front of the tablecloth forms its base.

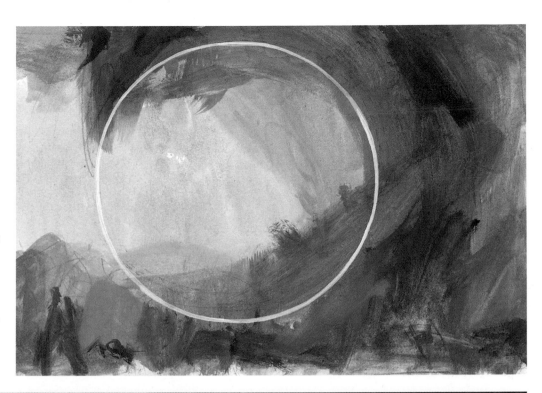

SNOWSTORM: HANNIBAL AND HIS ARMY CROSSING THE ALPS, *J.M.W. Turner* *This is Turner at his most dramatic, and shows an ingenious use of a circular compositional arrangement. The fact that the circle is incomplete, being suggested in the bottom left-hand corner by the area of shadow, together with the freedom with which it was painted, prevents the composition from becoming contrived.*

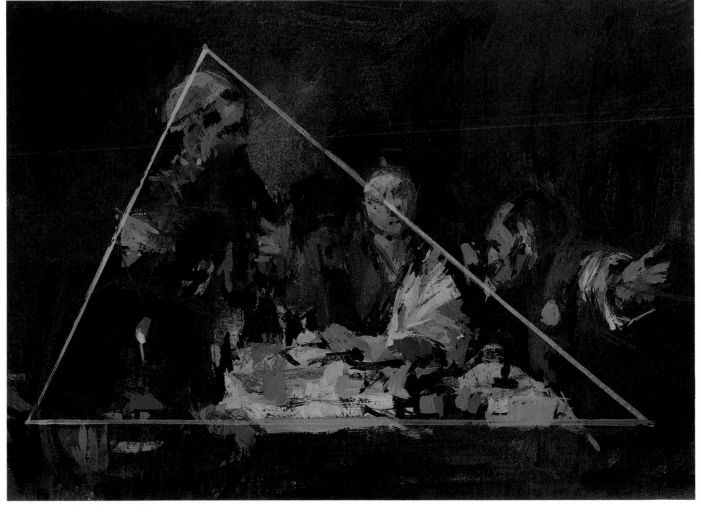

Colour

Colour can be used to create very exciting or very subtle effects, and can greatly enhance the finished effect of a drawing. You can take a different approach from painting, by using a very limited palette, deciding on a colour scheme that is distinctly different from reality, and experimenting with it. If you use a limited number of colours and mix them to produce intermediary colours, you will find it easier to control the colour effects in your work.

LIMITED PALETTE

When working with a limited range of colours, plan a colour scheme with three colours. Start by using variations on red, yellow and blue, and mix them to create intermediate colours and greys because they are too strong on their own. Have a selection of warm and cool reds, yellows and blues and one or two earth colours such as yellow ochre, and try out different combinations.

You can achieve compatibility of colour by mixing the colours you are using in this way. If you are using gouache or acrylics, mix the colours with some white so that all the colours you put down are within a similar tonal range.

For colour experiments, put down one colour as an overall background. Take another, stronger colour, mix in a little of the first colour plus white, which will bring the two colours closer together, and use this as your main drawing colour. Use the third colour with a little of the first two colours added to it, plus white. A fourth colour can be made from a mixture of the other colours you have used. Practise with each combination of colours until you get them working together.

Try experimenting with the following palettes for simple still lifes or landscapes. Gouache paint is best because it dries quickly, and if it dries on the palette, it just needs wetting to be usable again. Let each application of colour dry before adding another, or the first colour will be lifted off and the colours will start getting dirty. Also, mix up plenty of each colour so that you don't run out in the middle and have to spend time trying to match your colour mixtures.

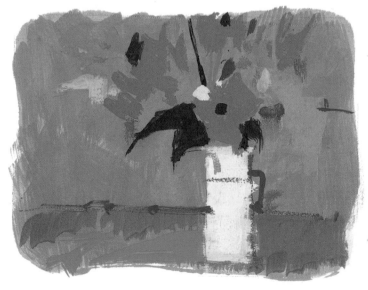

In this sequence, the flowers and vase were painted in the same colours throughout, but were set against different coloured backgrounds to show the way in which background colours affect the appearance of other colours. On a neutral grey background, the overall scheme tends towards cool colours. The leaves are a darkish brown, and the blue is also dark.

On a yellow-green background, the yellow and orange disappear, but the lilac flowers seem much brighter than they do against the grey. The blues are also stronger. Because this background is lighter than the blue and red backgrounds, the cream vase looks darker and duller in comparison.

Yellow ochre, cerulean blue and cadmium red light: use yellow ochre with a little white for the background colour, and mix a range of blues and greens to put over it.

Turquoise blue, magenta and cadmium yellow light: put down a strong turquoise background, and then mix the colours quite heavily to create subtle but bright hues to put down over it. Don't forget to add white to the mixtures as needed to keep them in a limited tonal range.

It is also interesting to try combinations of colours that are very close in hue, such as cobalt blue, cerulean blue and carmine red. Use touches of these colours mixed with quite a lot of white to get a range of very subtle colours, and try them over a blue background.

When a colour is applied over the initial background colour, the background colour will show through and affect the colour placed over the top – look for this as you experiment. If you use the colour quite wet over the background colour, it will bleed into the second colour and muddy it.

DO'S AND DON'TS

Do limit yourself to using only three or four colours in any drawing.

Do mix the colours you are using to produce interesting greys.

Do put down an overall background colour to unify the drawing and inspire you to get started.

Do mix up plenty of the colours you are intending to use so you don't have to spend time later trying to match colours.

Don't try to copy the whole range of colours you see in a subject.

Don't use just warm or cool colours in a drawing. Always use touches of a contrasting colour to set off the main colours..

Don't feel that you always have to use colour realistically. Choose a group of colours and match the intensity of colour rather than the actual colour.

On a turquoise background, the lilac stands out strongly, and so does the cream vase. The yellow and orange are intense, and the brown leaves appear lighter against this background than they do against the lighter grey and yellow-green backgrounds.

On the red background, the light blue is very intense, whereas against the grey background it looks darker. The brown leaves, which look dark against the grey background, look lighter against the red. By comparing the appearance of the same colours on these different backgrounds, you can see that colours change dramatically according to the colours they are placed against.

This grey/blue is at the cool end of the colour range and is a typical cool colour. It looks cool against any other colour, and even against white cartridge paper.

Green, a variant on blue, but slightly less cool because yellow has been added to the blue to create green.

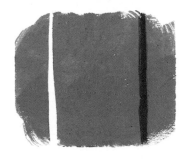

Beige – being in the middle of the cool/warm range, this kind of colour is much influenced by the colours next to it, looking cool next to reds and warm yellows, and warm next to blues and greens.

Orange – this is tending towards the warmer end of the range.

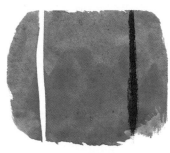

The hottest colour – orange/magenta – completes the scale. Warm colours have a greater intensity than cool colours. The white and dark bands demonstrate that a colour looks brighter against white than it does against a dark tone.

WARM AND COOL COLOURS

In relation to colour, warm and cool are relative terms because it depends what a colour is next to. On white paper, a colour is warm or cool as judged against the white.

What are called cool colours are usually in the colour range towards blue: warm colours are those tending towards orange-red. In between these two extremes are a multitude of hues that all affect each other when placed in proximity.

Warm colours tend to advance if they are next to cooler colours, and cool colours to recede when near warmer colours. As with tones, you can use this to create the effect of space.

SELECTIVE USE OF COLOUR

Rather than using colour in a naturalistic way, you can use it in a drawing purely to enhance the pencil or pen work.

You can use colour to balance a drawing. If a drawing has a large area of pencil or pen work, the line may be almost enough to stand on its own, but it might be improved by a wash of colour. If it is heavily worked in pencil or pen in places, strengthen the colour of the wash in emptier areas of the drawing, so that the colour balances the heavier line work and provides a foil for it.

It is also possible to map out areas of a drawing in colour. Instead of putting down a background colour and building on it afterwards, you can decide in advance what colours to put where, so that they will balance each other, and put them down directly. This is particularly effective when you are using watercolour, because you can suggest a sense of space by varying the tone of the wash in the sky and foreground. You can also map out areas of colour with a wash first, and then draw over them.

Cool light, blue/green washes were used from the sky down to the canal, over the buildings, with accents of red and yellow to balance the coolness and draw the eye to the main feature in the scene. The washes were also used to balance the pencil work. Against the heavier pencil line the colour has been strengthened, on the left of the drawing in the water to balance it. Areas of colour have been treated as an abstract pattern, and don't coincide with the outlines of the buildings.

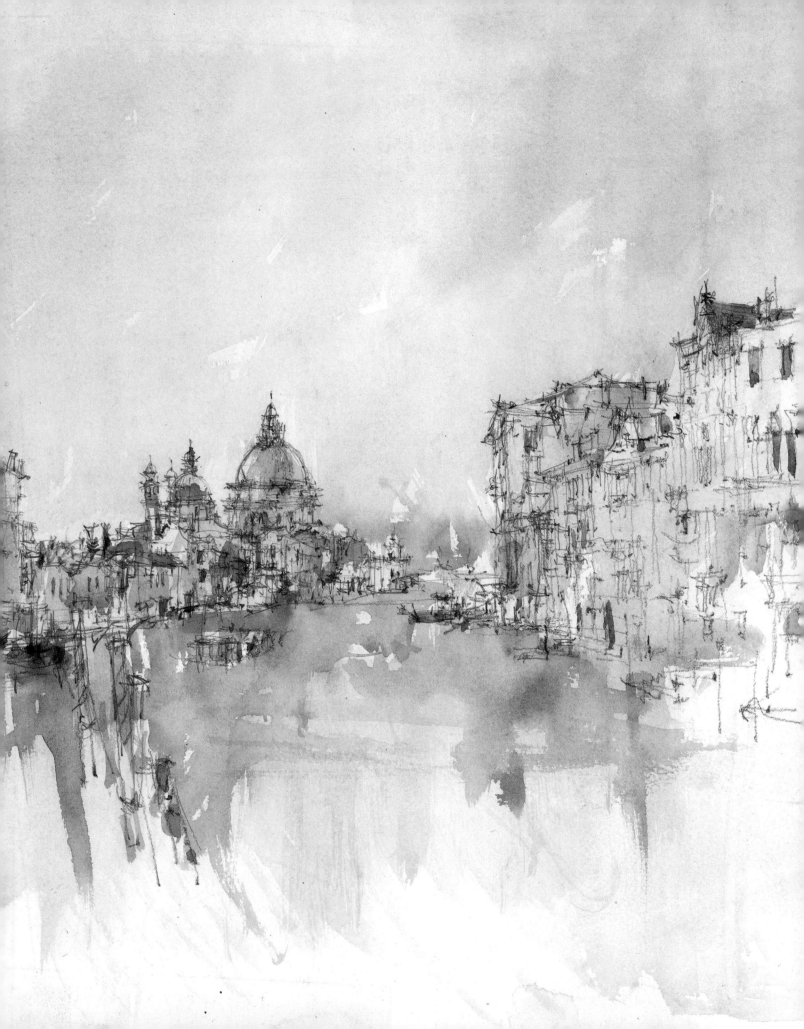

Practice

It is important to experiment with different colour effects. In these demonstrations, there are warm colours, cool colours, warm and cool together, light/dark contrasts and muted colours. Gouache is best for colour exercises, but you can introduce other media as well.

Try a drawing in a range of warm colours. Put down a very warm background, such as pink/red, and try both cool blue/greys and intense warm colours such as orange over it. The pink background showing through will have the effect of shifting the blue/grey towards a slightly warmer tint. Little touches of green/grey near the windmill intensify the reds.

Try an ochre/beige background in the middle of the warm/cool range and use cool and warm colours over the top. Here, predominantly warm colours have been used in the foreground, and the blues in the distance recede. The green is intensified by touches of red and white.

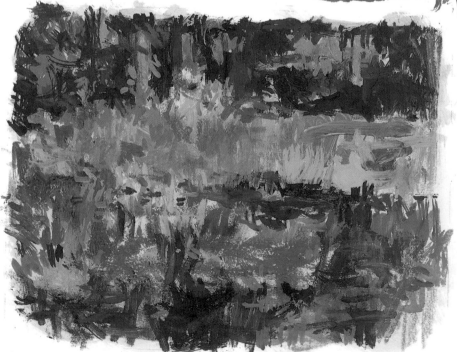

Strong light/dark contrasts in similar colours can create an interesting effect, especially when used on a bright background. Here the base colour is a yellow/green, and light blue and dark blue/grey have been used to create the main shapes in the subject, and are balanced by the mid-range greens across the middle of the drawing. The blues are slightly enhanced by the small red spots in the top left-hand corner.

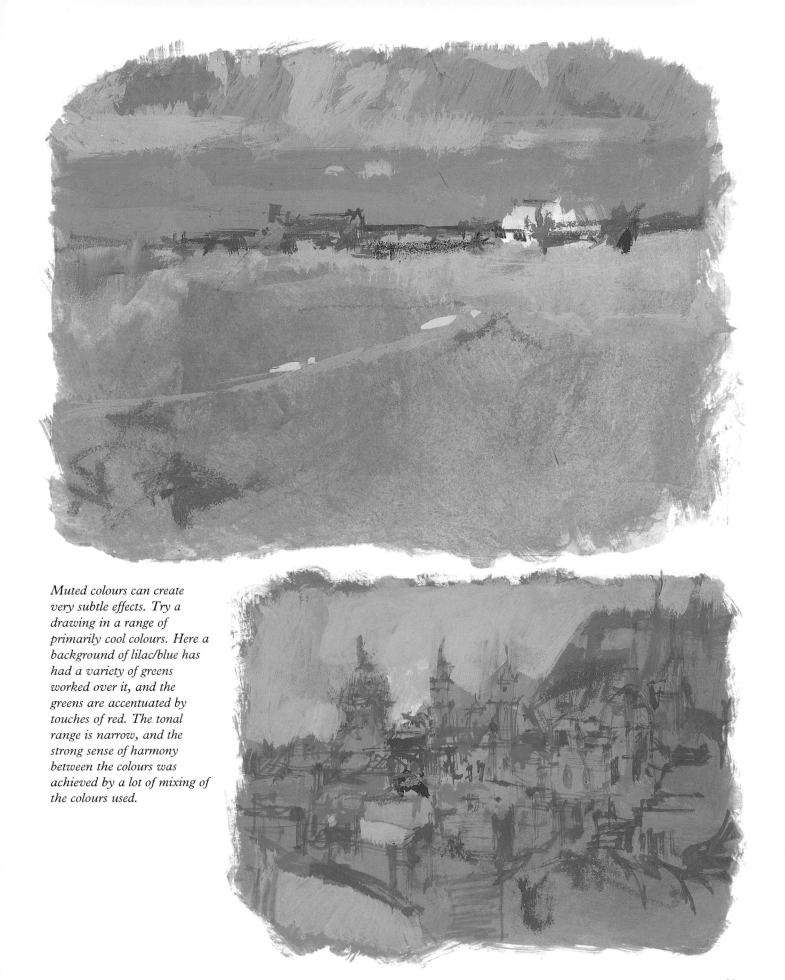

Muted colours can create very subtle effects. Try a drawing in a range of primarily cool colours. Here a background of lilac/blue has had a variety of greens worked over it, and the greens are accentuated by touches of red. The tonal range is narrow, and the strong sense of harmony between the colours was achieved by a lot of mixing of the colours used.

THE ELEMENTS

Wherever you are, and whatever you are doing, you are always surrounded by subjects. Get into the habit of carrying materials and a sketchbook with you all the time, and even if you only have 10 minutes to spare, sit down and sketch.

Tackle a variety of subjects to see which interests you most. Make some sketching excursions, and if you have a favourite place, see how many different ways you can draw it. Interpret subjects in a variety of materials and techniques, and work in different sizes and formats, to discover which suits you best. Eventually, you may find that you want to specialize in a particular type of subject matter and way of working, and this will form the basis of your own personal style.

Muted colours were washed on in gouache over cardboard, with accents of drawing in gouache to give the image some structure. Although this is unfinished, it needs no further work; the eye fills in the details.

People

Sooner or later you'll probably want to draw figures, either as a main subject or as part of a scene. To start with, try making thumbnail studies in a sketchbook to analyse the range of different positions that a figure can take up.

Take every opportunity to study people in all kinds of settings and engaged in all kinds of activities, whether you are drawing at the time or not. Analyse the overall shape that a figure creates, which will depend on stance, position, the way of sitting and so on. Note how the weight is balanced, the angle of the head and how the hands are held. If you are looking at groups, study the relationship between one figure and another. See how they overlap, and whether they bring their heads closer together when they are talking. If a group is seated, note how a standing figure will lean over them. Study the differences between a relaxed figure and one that is occupied with something.

DRAWING SINGLE FIGURES

When drawing individual figures, start with the head, because it is easier to fit a body on to a head than vice versa. When drawing a figure, don't concentrate on getting a likeness. Look instead at the angles within the figures, such as that of the head to the shoulders and body (page 38). By all means check that the proportions are correct by measuring (page 38), although this isn't always possible when you are making quick sketches. If drawing figures as reference material to put into other work, include some of the background because when you are back at home this will help you reproduce the correct proportions.

If you have not tried drawing figures before, start with people who are sitting, because this will give you more time, and practise drawing their overall shape. If you are using pencil, you can work over the drawing again and again, making changes and corrections. Don't bother about rubbing out because a multiple image can be more effective than a single one. And if the figure moves, just keep drawing.

The nearer parts of any subject will be larger in proportion to those further away – an effect known as foreshortening. You need to learn to see this by studying the relative sizes of different parts of the subject. Measuring can bring this out.

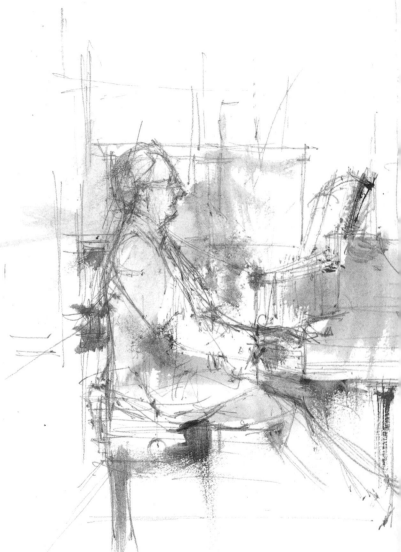

A unity of style has been achieved in these drawings of three different figures, done in pencil and wash. The overall shapes were drawn in pencil first, starting with the head in each case, and although the outlines are quite loose they demonstrate a knowledge of the figure. Very light washes were then applied so as not to destroy the pencil line. Important parts of the figures such as the head and legs of the seated figure, have been emphasized by leaving other areas unfinished.

In the figure above, the wash was applied in the background to emphasize the shape of the figure.

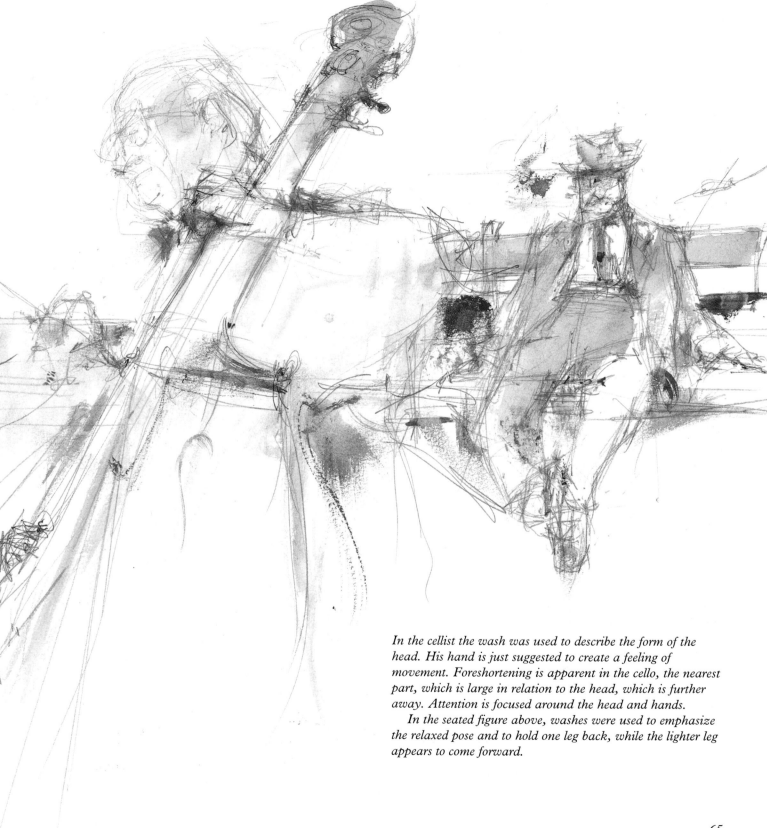

In the cellist the wash was used to describe the form of the head. His hand is just suggested to create a feeling of movement. Foreshortening is apparent in the cello, the nearest part, which is large in relation to the head, which is further away. Attention is focused around the head and hands.

In the seated figure above, washes were used to emphasize the relaxed pose and to hold one leg back, while the lighter leg appears to come forward.

GROUPS AND FIGURES IN SETTINGS

People give scale to a drawing, which is why it is important to include them. The smaller the people, the larger a building nearby will look.

When drawing a group, overlap the figures and try to create a sense of pattern by seeing how all the figures fit together. This will give the group unity. Also bear in mind that people vary in height, and a group will look more interesting if the heights of individuals within it are varied. If there are near and far figures in a scene, their eye-lines will be on the same level, allowing for variations in height. Their overall height will indicate their closeness or distance, so look for the position of their feet in relation to other figures and to their setting. Also, distant figures will be proportionately smaller than those that are in the foreground.

Figures are an intrinsic part of a setting, and should be treated in the same technique as the rest of the drawing. They should be integrated into the setting and sit happily within it.

In this gouache sketch of a bus queue, the emphasis is on capturing the overall shape of the group of people rather than producing a finished drawing. It was done on cardboard that had been given an overall wash to give unity to the sketch and make sure that the colours flowed well over it. The figures were blocked in with blue/greens and blue/greys over a creamy/grey background wash. None of the figures have been treated as an individual. Instead, they have all been seen and drawn in relation to each other. The head heights of the figures were varied in relation to the lines of the bus shelter, and the general pose of each figure was described. Colour splashes were added for the clothes. Once the overall effect and colouring had been captured, accents were added with a fine felt-tip pen to bring out details such as the tilt of the heads, the shapes of noses, the position of eyes and the placement of legs.

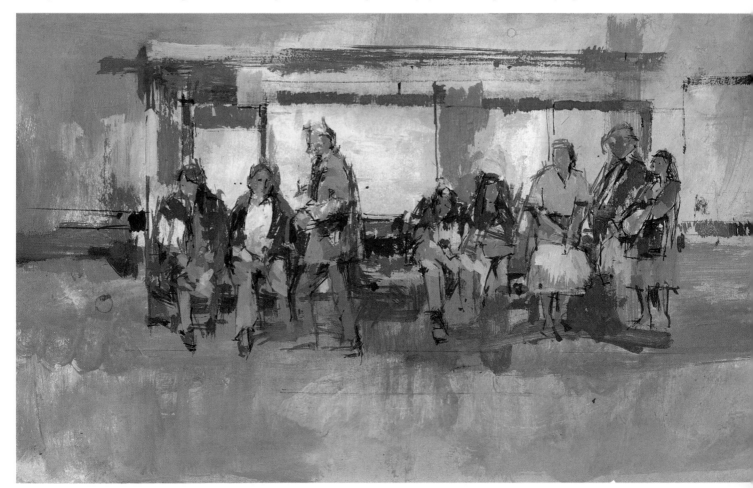

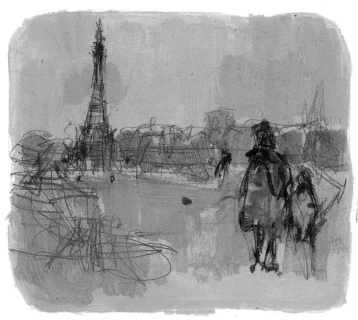

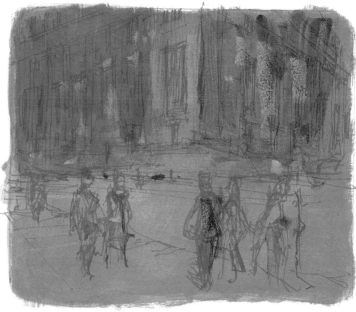

These figures are not exaggerated in proportion to the Eiffel Tower, but their height was utilized in relation to the distance so that they are not dominated by the scene. They were drawn in with brushwork and a matchstick to keep them simple.

Because only the bottom section of the building is visible, it seems to overpower the figures. And as the base of the building is at eye level in the drawing, it looks as if it is above the figures as well as being much bigger in proportion to them.

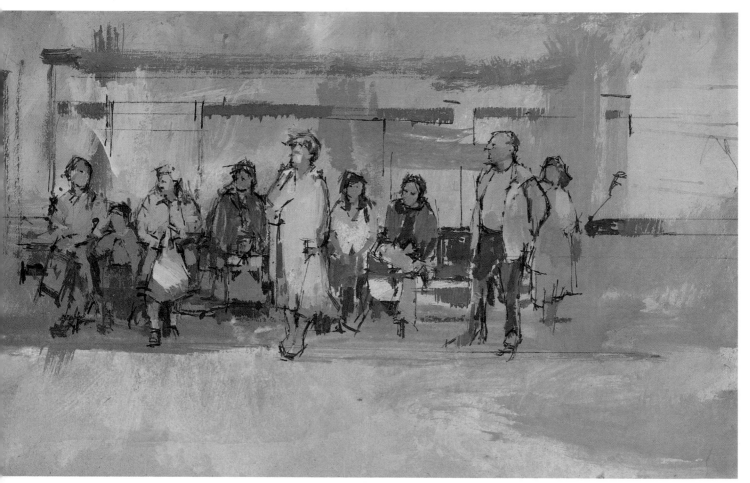

MOVEMENT

You don't need to be watching an all-action activity in order to draw movement. It is also the case that a moving figure often repeats certain positions, giving you a chance to capture them over a period of time. To begin with, try drawing people as they walk along the street. See how a person puts all their weight on one leg as they go forward, and how this is counterbalanced by the other leg trailing behind. Slow-motion replays on television provide a good opportunity to observe the extreme angles and unbalanced positions of people in action.

An impression of movement in a drawing is achieved through the dynamic angle and unbalanced position of a figure, and this can be exaggerated by the use of technique. Half-described, indistinct shapes, smudged pencil line and vigorous, rapid drawing can all help to suggest movement. The extreme angle of a moving figure should be contrasted with a stabilizing horizontal line in the background in order to emphasize it.

PORTRAITS

One of the worries of portraiture is in trying to get a likeness of the sitter, to the detriment of the drawing. You should try to capture the character rather than the likeness of the sitter, by observing the overall proportions of the head and the shapes of the individual features.

To start with, draw people you know well, as you will both feel more relaxed than if you're relative strangers. Once you've got a sitter, give them a comfortable seat that allows them to sit for quite a long time. They should have a break about every 20 minutes, and before they get up for the first time, mark the position of their shoulders, knees and feet with chalk on the chair and floor so that they can return to the same position.

Arrange the sitter's chair so that you are comfortable with the height, and make sure that you are both on the same eye-level. Keep the background simple, and check that the lighting gives the effect you want. Sidelighting creates a dramatic

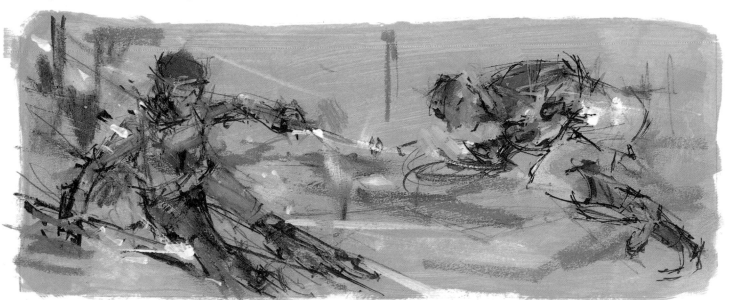

These two figures were drawn with pencil, crayon and gouache. Only the essential aspects of the figures are blocked in – the overall shape, the position of the arms, which balance the figures, and one or two details. Pencil lines reinforce the general direction in which the figures are moving, and the vigour of the drawing exaggerates the sense of movement. Lines in the background provide a stabilizing shape around each figure.

Right, these sketches were done mainly in pencil, with a little watercolour and pastel added afterwards. The angles of each figure were exaggerated so that their weight is very off-balance. None of them could remain still and not fall over. The pencil work was smudged to give the illusion of movement, and the watercolour washes were added to counterbalance the positions of the figures. Horizontal and vertical lines have been included to emphasize the angles of the figures.

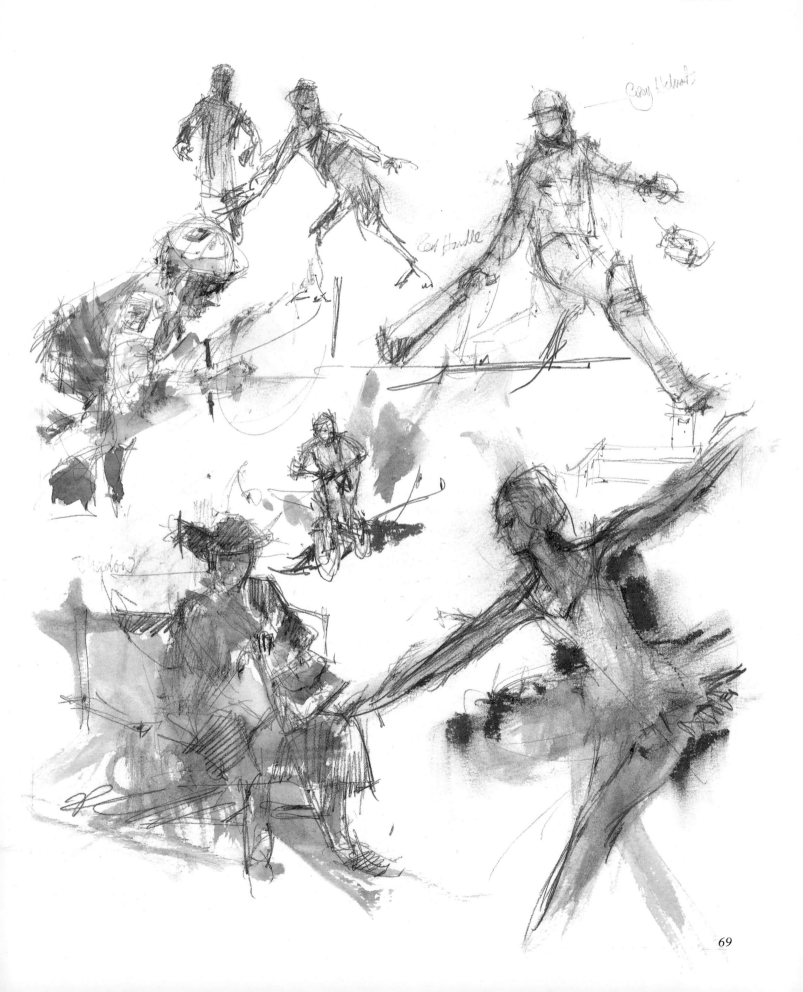

effect, whereas indirect lighting is softer.

Before you start, walk all round the sitter to make sure that you have chosen the most interesting position.

STRUCTURE OF THE HEAD

Start by outlining the shape of the skull. You can put in a line down the centre of the face to give you the tilt of the head, and then put in a line for the angle of the eyes. Then check the overall proportions of the head by measuring (page 38). You can make measuring marks on the drawing if you want, and they can be left in to become part of the finished work. Compare the distances from the hair-line to the top of the nose, from the top of the nose to the tip of the nose, and from the tip of the nose to the tip of the chin. Then check the hair-line to the top of the nose in relation to a horizontal taken from the top of the nose to the side of the skull.

Once you have got the overall proportions, you can concentrate on the shapes of the different features and their position in relation to each other. The eyeball is a sphere set in a socket in the skull.

Observe how the shadows under the brow and under the eye itself create the shape of the eye socket. This is one of the most important elements in conveying the character of the sitter. The shape of the nose is created by the shadow on either side of it – the shadow is usually stronger on one side than the other – and by the shadow under the tip of the nose.

The angle of the mouth is dictated by the tilt of the head, and should be the same as that of the eyes. To get the width of the mouth, note where the sides of the mouth come below the eyes. The shape of the mouth is captured through the lines of the cheeks from the sides of the nose to the sides of the mouth. The chin is a very subtle shape, best shown through the strong shadows under it. To determine the position of the ears, note where the top and bottom of the ears come in relation to the eyes and nose. And bear in mind that even if the head is tilted, the neck is vertical.

To capture the character of your sitter, observe the various subtleties in the shapes of their features. Decide which is the most characteristic feature, and emphasize it slightly.

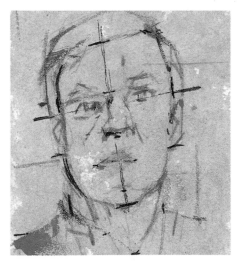 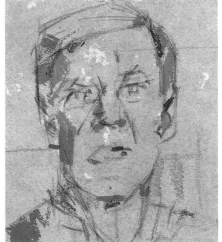 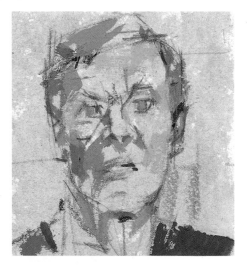

First the basic shape of the head was outlined. Then the different parts of the head were measured against each other to establish the correct proportions. The tilt of the head and the angle of the eyes were drawn in to establish the correct relationship between the eyes and the nose. The neck is vertical.

Once the overall drawing was established, areas of tone were added down one side of the face and under the nose and chin to describe the general shape of the head, using cool colours. Marks were made on the hair to establish the tone in that area, and in the background.

Warmer flesh colours were added for the mid-tones, to establish the overall tonal range. Shadow was added on either side of the nose to establish its shape. A mid-grey was used on the eyes. The cool tones were carried down the side of the cheek and under the chin, and colour was added to the clothes.

COLOUR

Although a great range of subtle colours can be seen in flesh tones, it is best to use a limited palette. Use cooler colours in the shadow areas and a lighter flesh colour over the rest of the face – for mid tones and highlights. Don't make the hair too strong a colour. It should be compatible with the tones in the face. Bear in mind that when you put in the background, it will change the colours in the face. It is best to keep the background in key with the tones in the face, and to develop both simultaneously. Don't make the white of the eyes too white. Again they should be within the tonal range of the rest of the face. And the lips, also, should not be too bright. If anything, underplay colour in the face.

Use the same style in the clothes as in the rest of the drawing, and again keep them within the same tonal range.

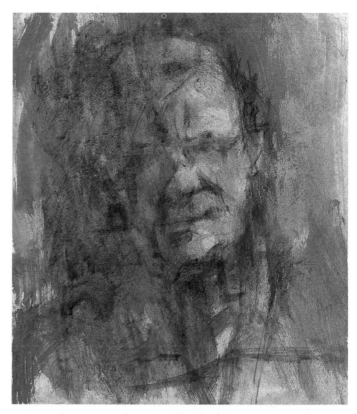

Right, a loose monochrome study of a head using the texture and grain of the paper in the background. Scumbled browns and greys were used to create the main shadow areas across the head and background. Chalk was then added to emphasize the shape of the head.

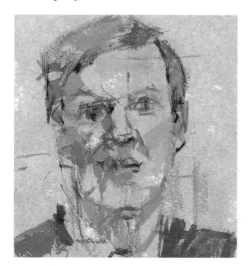

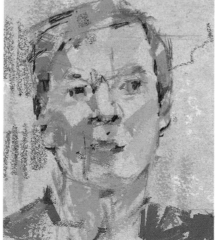

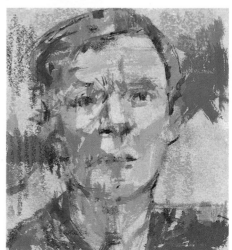

More modelling was added under the eye and on the side of the nose, to create more specific and accurate shapes. More drawing was done around the mouth and touches of deeper tones were added around the head. A touch of warmer colour was added under the chin to create reflection.

Part of the background was filled in to establish its relationship with the head. More emphasis was added to the eyes and nose, and stronger accents were added around the edges of the head. A touch of bright orange was added to the left-hand shoulder to create vibrancy and set off the cooler colours.

The background was developed further on the right-hand side, and more work was done around the eyes, nose and mouth. Tones were carried across from the background to the head to create unity and make the head sit within the picture. All parts of the drawing have been worked in the same style.

Practice

Make mental notes and observations about people all the time, and study them even when you are not drawing them. When drawing individuals remember to concentrate on getting the shapes correct rather than on drawing a likeness, and keep correcting a drawing as you observe more accurately.

Try a straightforward pencil study of a head, using a 2B pencil. Observe the relationships between different parts of the head, and make heavier marks at the hairline to exaggerate the line of the forehead. If the person wears glasses, draw them in. They give you the line from the eye to the ear; and the line across the brow gives you the tilt of the head.

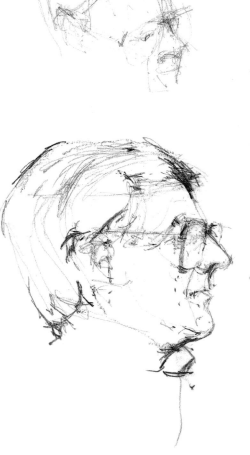

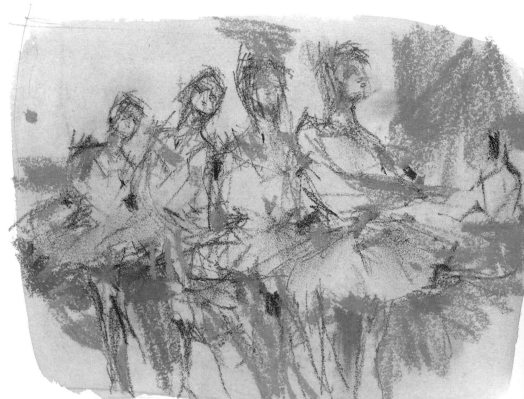

DO'S AND DON'TS

Do take every opportunity to study the way people look and move.

Do measure to check the overall proportions of your subject, whether drawing the whole figure or doing a portrait.

Do include some of the background, and draw it in the same style as the figure so that the two are integrated.

Do overlap figures in groups, and see a group as an overall pattern rather than as a collection of individuals.

Don't try to draw a likeness in a portrait, draw the head as a series of interelated shapes.

Don't worry about making mistakes, just keep working over what you have already done. And don't bother to tidy up structural or wrong marks.

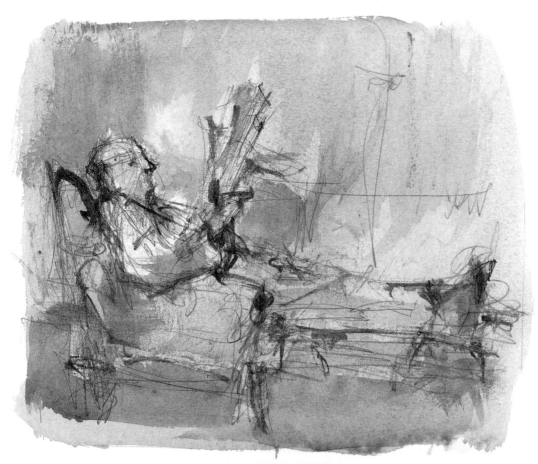

Left, if someone is settled in front of the television or reading a book, you have an opportunity to try a more time-consuming medium. Try pen and wash, drawing the basic shapes with pen first, and then adding a wash to emphasize the form of the figure. Work as quickly as possible because nothing in the drawing needs to be very distinct, although the important features should be a little more clearly defined.

Below, a group can be drawn in pencil to start with, and a wash added later – as was the case here. When drawing a group study how the figures knit together.

Left, draw a group of figures, concentrating on seeing them in relation to each other. Notice how angles such as the tilt of shoulders create an overall pattern.

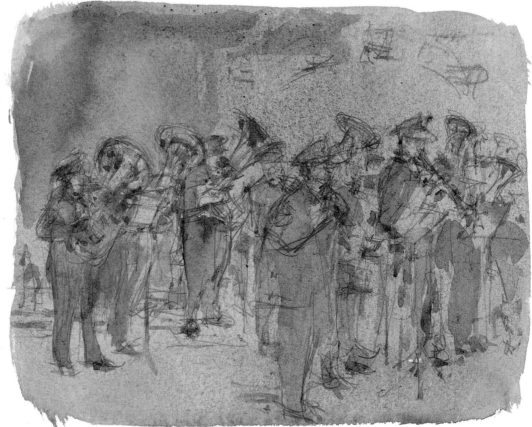

Animals

Animals can provide endless variety as a subject for drawing. It teaches you to observe structure, and the range of textures, colours and patterns offer plenty of scope for experimenting with different techniques. One of the challenges of drawing animals is to create a sense of the fur or feathers without drawing them in.

If you have pets at home, try drawing them. Some cats will even pose for you. Make quick notes of the animal's overall shape and characteristic features, such as the way the tail curls underneath it. Horses are difficult but are a good test of your powers of observation. The hind legs in particular will need careful study.

Farm animals are easily accessible for many people. Cows are interesting to draw because they have a pleasing overall shape – and they keep reasonably still. Pigs give a touch of hilarity, and a challenge in conveying their bulk. With geese, the main thing is to try to capture their character.

Of the birds, cockerels are a good subject as they are a striking shape, and they tend to pose. Parrots are fun because of their distinctive shapes and the wonderful colours and patterns of their plumage. Seagulls have attractive colours and soft, downy feathers and distinctive hooked beaks.

A zoo is also a good place for drawing animals. Whatever your subject, look for its individual characteristics and emphasize them. Elephants have great bulk and distinctive ears. Ostriches and orang-utans provide humour, and the giraffe is a good

example of an animal dominated by pattern.

Start by looking at the overall proportions of the animal: the size of the head in relation to the body; the length of the body; the angle and length of the legs. Study the shape and tilt of the head; the way the animal holds its tail; and the way that it walks. Then try drawing the outline of the animal in one continuous line in order to observe its shape. You can measure the subject in order to get the proportions correct (page 38), and you could include some of the background in order to give a sense of scale. Alternatively, you could show the animal in its natural habitat. If it is well camouflaged in its natural environment, you can use this to create atmosphere and pattern in the drawing.

FUR AND FEATHERS

If you are drawing with pencil, use the pencil line to indicate the direction of growth of the fur, but not all over the animal. Use it to emphasize the shape of the animal in key places such as around the head and shoulders, and under the body.

Gouache is a good medium to work in if you want to capture the texture of fur or feathers. First put down a background wash. Then create the overall shape of the animal using a dry brush and thick paint to give an impression of fur, varying the colour slightly. You can finally add in a few fine lines for individual hairs to add accents.

The character of the dog on the left is captured through the tilt of the head and the perkiness of its tail. The cat has been drawn in general outline rather than being highly observed, which conveys its relaxed pose. On the right is a study of the construction of a dog's head.

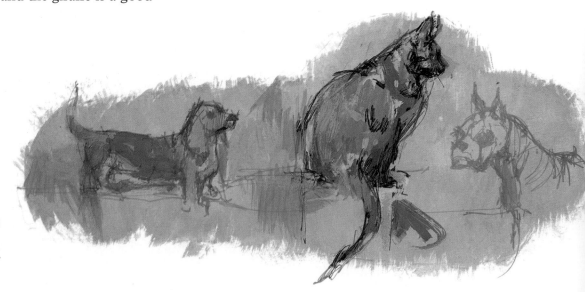

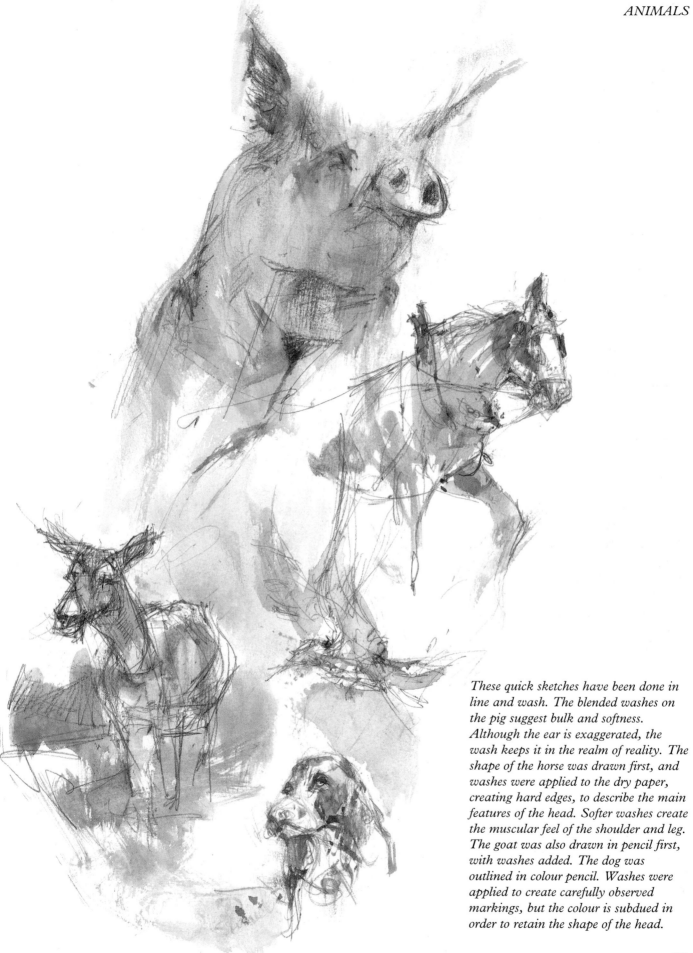

These quick sketches have been done in line and wash. The blended washes on the pig suggest bulk and softness. Although the ear is exaggerated, the wash keeps it in the realm of reality. The shape of the horse was drawn first, and washes were applied to the dry paper, creating hard edges, to describe the main features of the head. Softer washes create the muscular feel of the shoulder and leg. The goat was also drawn in pencil first, with washes added. The dog was outlined in colour pencil. Washes were applied to create carefully observed markings, but the colour is subdued in order to retain the shape of the head.

PATTERN

Don't draw in every spot or stripe. Observe where the most distinctive ones are and use them to create the essence of the animal. You can also use pattern to emphasize the form of the animal. However, use it selectively so that it does not become dominant and destroy the shape of the animal.

Because pattern is such a strong characteristic of some animals, it can be suggested by putting down the pattern over an area that is roughly the right shape, and then doing a little drawing over it to suggest one or two telling features such as a tail or an eye. In this case, don't draw in the outline, let the pattern identify the animal.

It isn't possible to describe both texture and pattern. You need to decide which is most characteristic of the animal and include just that.

TECHNIQUES

Pencil is excellent for drawing animals because you can work over the drawing again and again. Charcoal is also good, because it enables you to observe and capture the bulk of an animal through simple shapes. If you want to try pen and wash, draw the general shape first with pen, then emphasize the individual characteristics of the animal, such as its beak, ears or a large head, by drawing them in more strongly. Then use a light wash to emphasize the shape through shadows on the animal.

Colour pencils can be used to make rapid colour notes. For more considered drawings, you can select a colour appropriate to the animal.

Spattering and sponging can be used to create texture in selected areas, but in order to do this you will need to mask out the other areas of the drawing with card.

MOVEMENT

Movement can be created through indistinctness, overlaying lines rather than going for a clear shape. It can also be suggested by softening or fading out the parts, such as legs, that are moving. Areas of smudging can also convey action. The animal or the background can be blurred. Either will suggest that the animal is moving.

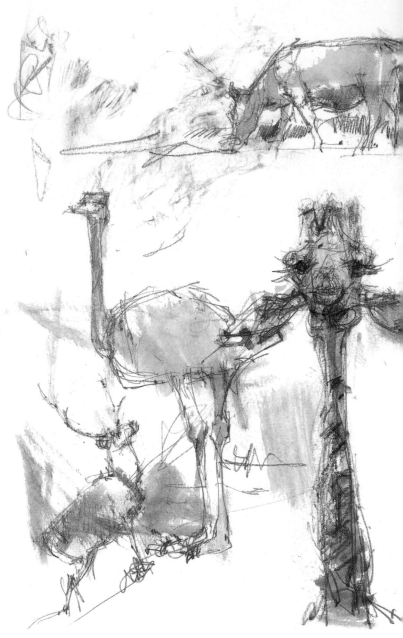

Above, these loose studies were done mainly with pencil and wash. Pencil was used to create the general shapes of each animal, and light washes were then added to emphasize the shape. Pattern was loosely added in some cases with pencil, such as on the giraffe. Notice that the toad's warts were drawn in over a small area only. Dark washes were used on the cormorant's neck to accentuate the shape of its head. In the case of the leopard, the pattern was sponged on, and some spots were emphasized with red ink. The orang-utan was drawn in with conté pencil, and light washes were added to create the shape of the body.

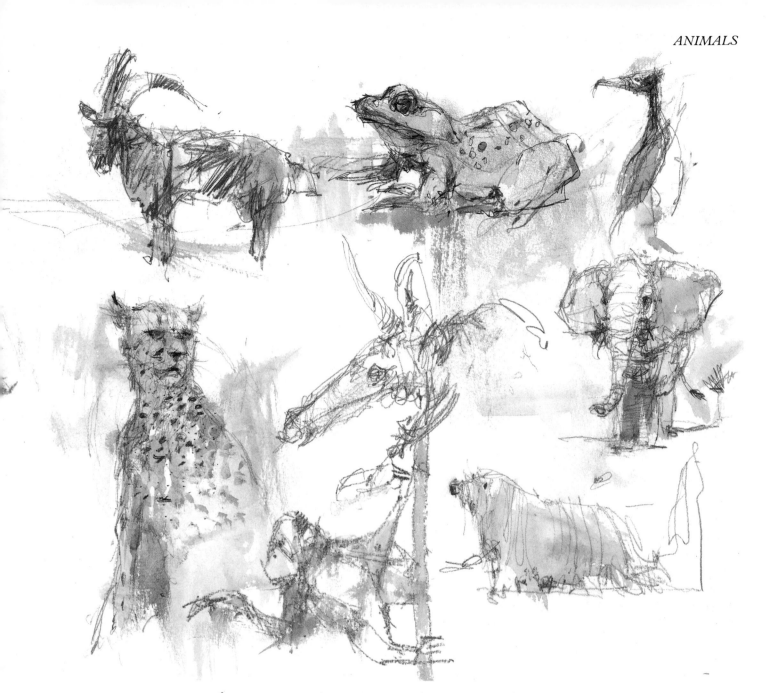

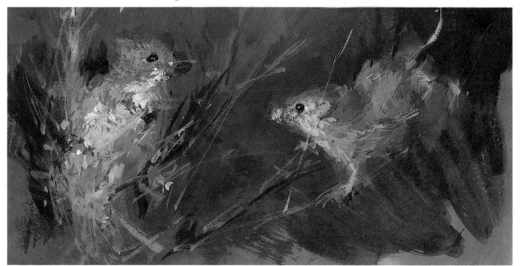

Left, in this gouache sketch, heavier colour was applied over a wash background. The texture of the fur was created by blocking in the general shape of the animals with dry brushstrokes. Details were then painted in here and there with a fine brush.

Practice

Try lots of approaches to animals – pencil, watercolour, colour pencils and pens, line and wash. Be clear in your own mind why you are doing a drawing – whether to make a carefully observed study or just a fleeting impression based on pattern, colour and general shape.

Whatever the purpose of the drawing, put up the animal in some kind of setting to give it a sense of scale, and give the background a similar treatment. Humour can be an important part of a drawing of an animal. Try to identify its characteristic features, and exaggerate them slightly.

Use washes to capture an animal in its setting. You only need to observe one part of the animal in detail – here the distinctive markings on the badger's head. Put a wash on all over and while it is still damp, start flooding in colour to create a soft shape that blends into the background. Any strong markings can be added once the wash is dry.

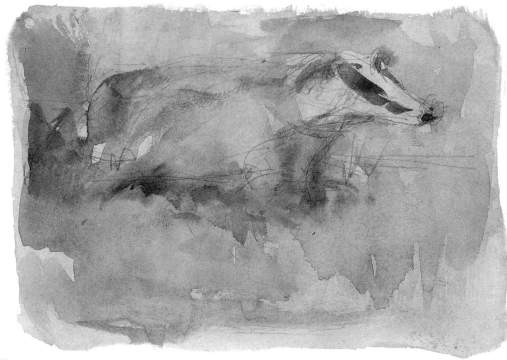

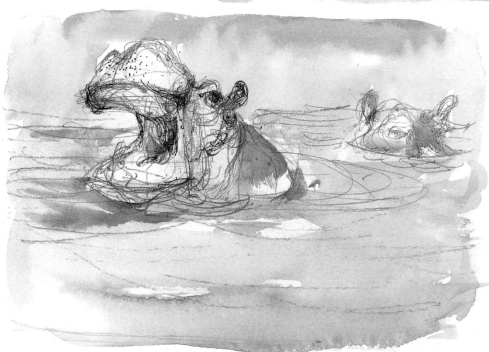

Make a drawing that emphasizes the main characteristic of an animal – in this case the hippo's huge mouth – and put it in its setting. Pencil, wash and pen were used for this illustration. First pencil was used to draw the head of the hippo in a continuous flow of lines. The wash was applied leaving windows for the highlights. Pen can be used to create the shadows.

Try using line only to create
the sense of an animal's fur,
without drawing it in detail.
Follow the direction of the
coat around the head,
shoulders, arms and under
the body to create the form of
the animal.

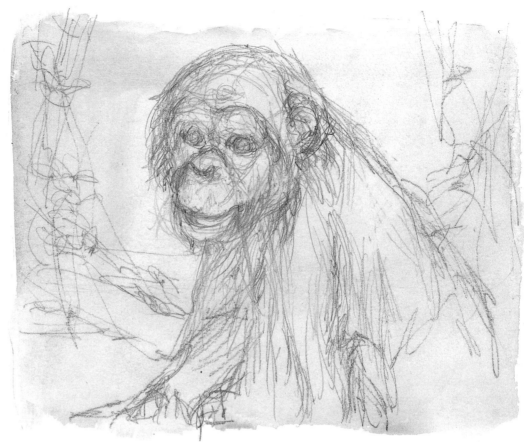

Try to create a sense of
movement in a rapid, sketchy
felt-tip pen drawing. Just
doodle, and move all over the
shapes of the animals; don't
draw any outlines. You can
try adding a loose wash over
a small area on top of the
drawing approximately where
the shadows are on the
subject.

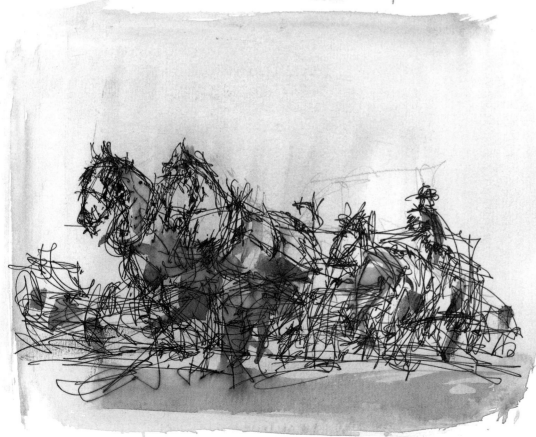

Flowers and Still Life

Flowers and still-life objects are excellent subjects to set up at home. They provide an endless variety of shapes, colours and textures to study, and can be left in a corner and returned to again and again.

FLOWERS

Like any object, flowers conform to a geometric shape – circle, sphere, ellipse, cone and so on – and this can help in the construction of the drawing. Flower drawing also provides the opportunity to use colour in an imaginative way and to enjoy the patterns created by leaves and petals.

Select a flower such as a chrysanthemum or dahlia, and note its basic geometric shape. Also study the way in which the flower is supported by the stem, and the pattern of the leaf growth. Note the shape of any buds. They are not just smaller versions of the flowers, but have a compact shape of their own. Within one flower there are many different shapes that you can use against each other.

Analyse the shape of each petal and see how it contributes to the form of the whole flower. Then build up the shape of the flower petal by petal. However, although you need to observe the petals individually, you need to draw them as one, keeping the line going so that they are all linked into a whole.

The overall colour of a flower is affected by the way shadow falls across it and describes its shape. See how the light catches one side of the flower, and how it casts shadow across individual petals. Look for accents of shadow within the flower as this describes its form. Also see how the turn of a leaf can cast another shadow.

This was a disciplined exercise using a 2B pencil. The structure of the flowers was carefully observed, although they were freely drawn. The basic shape of each flower – circular, spherical, heart-shaped and so on – was sketched in first to provide a guideline to work within, and the flowers were then built up petal by petal.

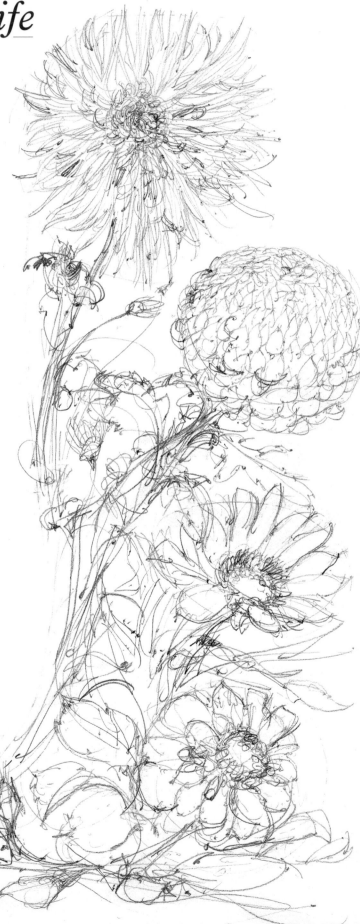

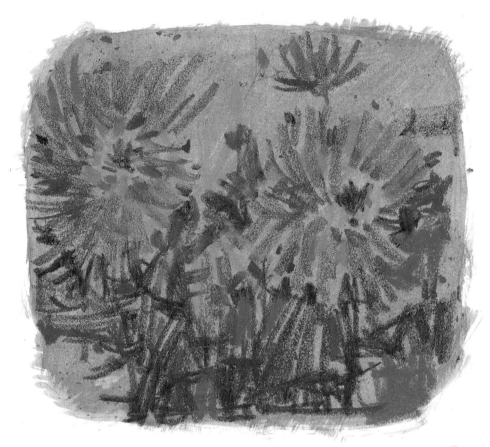

Left, this pastel study is an example of pattern-making with flowers. First the position of each flower was planned. Then the flower heads were created with rapid strokes directed towards the centre of the flowers. Similar marks were used, but closer together, for the leaves and stalks to create a denser effect. Dashes of blue were added to relieve the overall colour effect.

Below, in this watercolour study direct painting was combined with areas where the colours were allowed to flow. This can be done by slightly dampening areas where you want this effect before applying colour, and using hard-edged washes to form the shapes of some petals.

TECHNIQUES

Pencil is a good medium for flower studies. It is important to keep the pencil line flowing over the whole flower. Use a wrist movement to create the flow of the drawing through the petals, leaves and stalks.

Watercolour is particularly good for capturing an impression of a flower. Block in the overall shape, but do not put in each petal individually. If you want to describe an individual petal, alter the tint of the wash slightly. Within the flower leave windows in the wash for highlights, and add an accent of colour in the centre of the flower. Use the tone and colour of the leaves to intensify the brilliance of the flowers.

Pastel is probably the best medium for flowers. You do not always need to use too much variety of colour in flowers, and pastel will stop you being too ambitious. It also forces you to describe shape and colour in one stroke. This is best achieved by applying the colour with vigorous strokes, using the leaves to create a pattern that works against the flowers.

SETTING UP A STILL LIFE

When choosing objects for a still life, keep the shapes as simple as possible, and utilize basic shapes such as circles and cubes. Try to select things with a linking characteristic such as their shape or the material they are made from, or choose things within a limited range of colour.

When arranging a still life, keep some height in the background, as this helps to create an overall shape, but do not use something that is much taller than everything else. Bear in mind the compositional shapes described earlier (page 50). A triangular composition is particularly effective for a still life. Don't treat the objects as individual items and set them up in isolation from each other. Rather, arrange them to create an overall shape. To do this, overlap the objects so that they connect with each other visually. Also think about the arrangement of the objects in relation to the frame of the drawing, because the spaces around the objects are as important as the objects themselves.

DRAWING A STILL LIFE

Still life provides a very good discipline in getting the basic drawing correct through studying the relationships of one thing to another. Plan the still life on paper first if you want, set it up, and then interpret it back on to paper again. Whatever the different elements in the still life, try to create a

---

DO'S AND DON'TS

Do see flowers as basic geometric shapes.

Do observe the shape and structure of different parts of a flower, but draw it as one.

Do note the way in which cast shadows alter the colours of flowers.

Do set up a still life to make an overall shape, and draw it by seeing the objects in relation to one another.

Don't copy patterns in the background, just give an impression of them.

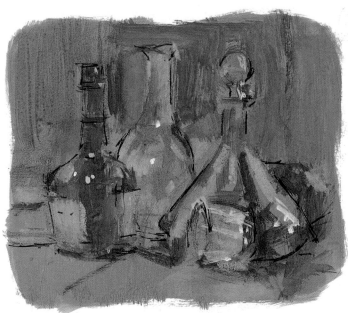

Above, two decanters, a glass and bottle, arranged in a triangular composition, with a fairly simple overall background. Front lighting cast highlights on the fronts of the bottles and minimum shadow. Simplified masses of colour and a limited tonal range were used, accentuated by highlights on the glass.

Left, an alternative set-up using the same objects, based on a diagonal composition. This time they were arranged against the light, giving heavy shadows and luminosity in the glass. The shadows form an important part of the composition.

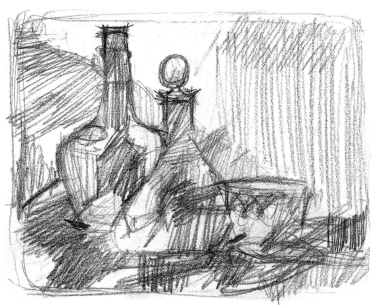

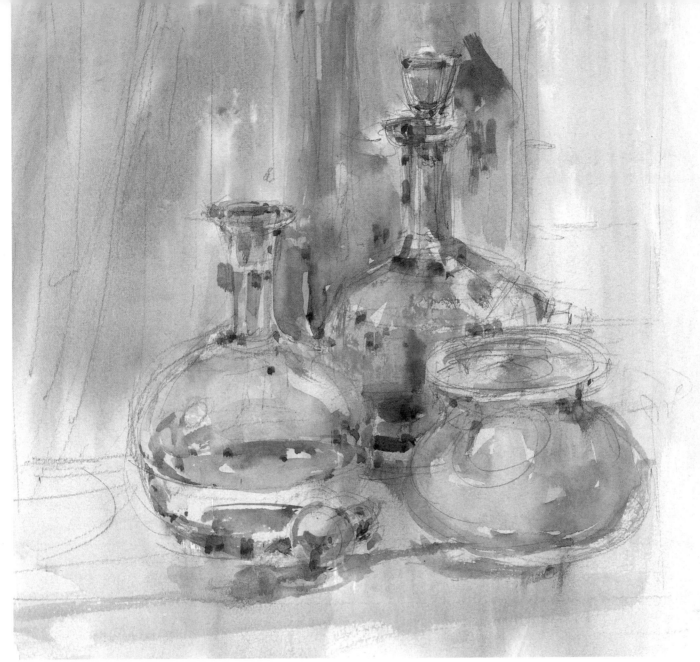

Pencil and wash were used to bring out the transparent quality of the glass containers within the overall style of the drawing. The paper was tinted before starting, and the washes were applied as quickly as possible so that the edges of some were softened by the wet paper. Observed highlights were created by leaving areas of white paper.

The patterned fabric in the background was put in with an overall wash, and subtle changes of tone and colour were used to suggest its presence. The maximum number of washes used on any area of the drawing was three.

pattern across the whole drawing through using a consistent style for the objects and the background.

First work out the proportions of the main object and then work out the position and sizes of the other objects in relation to the first. You can measure the subject to get the relative proportions (page 38). Also check that you have got any angles correct. Build up the drawing from the points of contact between objects, and between the objects and the background. And see where you can use perpendiculars or horizontals in the background to plot the relative positions of the objects.

Be selective about the way in which you include a pattern on the background fabric. Use it to describe the contours of the fabric, but don't slavishly copy the pattern.

Practice

It is worth spending time experimenting with different still-life set-ups, trying different compositional arrangements and making quick sketches of them. Also try sketching the same set-up from different distances and viewpoints. Compare the results to see which arrangements create the most striking effects, which create a flat effect and which have depth.

Good objects include vases, bottles, cups and saucers, plates and bowls, containers, drink cans, wine glasses and tumblers, books, paints and brushes; natural objects such as fruit, shells and pebbles; tools, garden implements and kitchen utensils. You can combine flowers and plants with simple objects, which provides an interesting contrast between complex and simple forms.

For a background you can use curtains, tablecloths, cushions, or even old clothes. Build up a collection of different colours and patterns, and also look for materials with a distinctive texture, such as open-weave fabrics or satin.

Still-life drawing will help with all other subjects because it provides a good opportunity to study simple, basic forms and to practise keeping lines parallel, circles and ellipses symmetrical, verticals upright, and so on. You can work fast, or make more considered, measured drawings. If you feel sufficiently confident, you can include part of the room setting.

See the subject in terms of abstract shapes, and remember to use the same technique for subject and background so that they are integrated. Establish the overall proportions within the drawing and then rough out the basic shapes of the objects. To give the impression that one object is stepped behind another, notice where one object strikes another and build up the drawing by moving from one of these points to the next.

Still-life subjects are also good for experimenting with different materials and effects. Use them to try out high-key and low-key tonal treatments, and different limited-colour palettes. You could also try a variety of mixed-media effects.

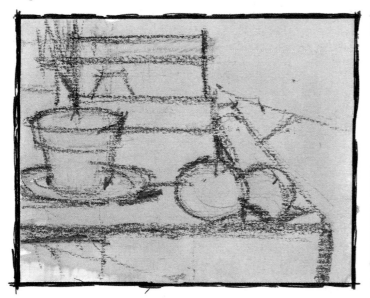

Take a selection of objects and experiment with moving them around in order to create different relationships between the objects in terms of size and shape. Here a flower-pot, a box and some fruit were chosen because they represent the basic shapes of a circle and a square.

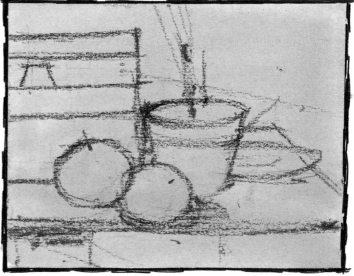

Try arranging the objects first in a diagonal arrangement, left, and then in a triangular arrangement, above. In the sketch above, although the pot is in the centre, the box on the left prevents the arrangement being too symmetrical. Sketch both your set-ups and see which you prefer.

For a more complex exercise, set up a still life with flowers and interpret it with mixed media giving all the elements the same treatment. Working on a coloured background, first draw in the outlines of the main shapes in pencil or felt-tip pen. Then block in the shapes – objects and background – with gouache. Bright touches of colour, such as flowers, can be touched in with oil pastel and line work can be emphasized if necessary with felt-tip pen.

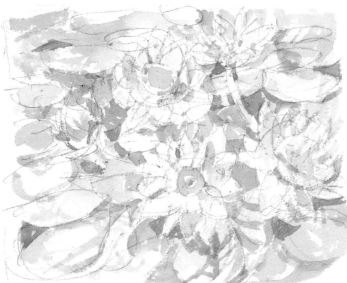

Select a small bunch of flowers and instead of looking at them as objects, try to see them as a pattern, with no part being too dominant. First break down the overall shape into a pattern with simple pencil lines, positioning them on the paper. Then mix up a light-coloured wash and build up each flower with small blocks of colour.

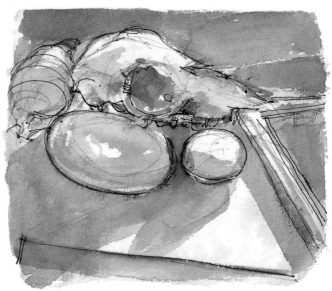

Set up a still life using natural objects that are similar in colour and tone – here a selection of pebbles, shells and a skull have been used. Arrange the still life so that the shadows cast by the objects are as interesting as the objects themselves and help to lead the eye around the picture. Then draw the set-up treating objects, shadows and background in the same way.

Landscape

A landscape can be far too large to cope with in one drawing. It is better to take sections or details, and make several drawings rather than one. Landscape can be approached using any medium, although there is a great tradition of using watercolour. It is made up of several elements, and it is worth looking at each separately.

SKY

Sky is the most variable aspect of a landscape. It is a good idea to keep a small sketchbook just for skies, making studies and notes of different types of clouds, rainbows, weather effects and colour, using pencil and watercolour. Sky should be seen in relation to the landscape, so always include a simple indication of the landscape.

When studying clouds, the biggest problem is the speed at which they move. To cope with this, decide what effect or arrangement you want to get down prior to starting, and stick to that. Look for the forms within clouds, which are created by light and shadow. Shafts of light piercing the clouds can be difficult to convey. Try to get down the overall effect of the sky first, and then suggest the shafts of light by rubbing out.

If you are working in colour try to get away from blue skies. You can translate the sky into any colour as long as you keep to the same intensity of colour as you see in the sky itself.

When using pencil, it may be more effective to suggest the shapes within the clouds, rather than filling in the areas of sky between the clouds. Charcoal is excellent for studies of skies because you can create effects quickly by smudging. Conté is good used lightly to suggest drifting, whispy clouds. If you are using pen and wash, limit the amount of pen work in the sky.

Watercolour is ideal for skies, because you can work very quickly with it, getting an airy, watery feel by applying a simple wash. You can also use a combination of hard and soft edges around clouds. Gouache can be used as a background wash with opaque paint applied over it, letting some of the background show through. Pastel is ideal for skies, especially on coloured paper. It can be smudged for a soft effect, or used strongly.

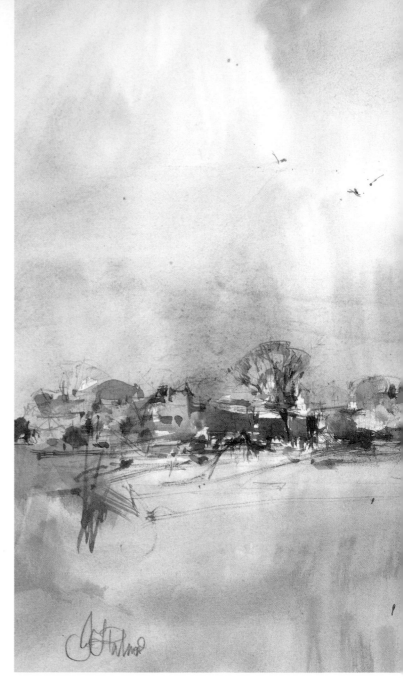

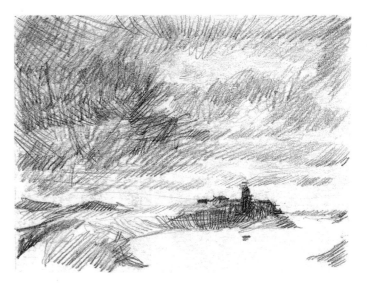

This was done in pencil and wash with the sky occupying over half of the drawing area. The right-hand trees provide a link between foreground and sky. The scene was sketched in first. Then the paper was dampened so that the washes would be softened. An overall cream wash was applied first, and blue and grey were put on over the top in the sky area, producing a random, luminous, watery effect. The horizon was then strengthened by stronger washes and more distinct forms.

Left, pencil was used to create bands of tone, giving weight to different areas within the sky, and creating strength and contrast against the horizon. The whole effect has been achieved by diagonal strokes and crosshatching, leaving bands of white in between.

Right, pastel and gouache were used to give the effect of a heavy sky. Mid-toned and dark shapes were blocked in with a light-toned background wash to create bulky clouds. The horizon, which is low, has been suggested with touches of colour.

WATER

Water in a landscape provides an interesting contrast to the features around it. Because it reflects the sky and the things round about, it can provide a splash of colour and liven up a scene.

One of the most important characteristics of water is the surface reflections. They are larger than you may think, and extend further than you may think, so study them carefully. They match fairly faithfully the tones and colours of the things being reflected. If there is any surface movement, the reflections will be broken up and become more abstract. Also notice the way that reflections of shadows under objects are elongated, and that reflections of shadows are not dark because they are also reflecting blue in the sky.

If the surface is rippled, try to break it down into a pattern. This pattern will keep repeating, giving you a chance to capture it. Make pencil studies of the surface patterns, trying to sketch them as quickly as possible. Gouache is the best paint medium for quick studies. Put on a darker colour, and scumble a lighter colour (but not white) over it.

TREES

Pick trees that have an interesting shape and are well balanced. A good time to draw them is when they have lost their leaves – bear in mind that dead trees can be as interesting to draw as living ones because of their stark shapes and the fact that they stand alone. Don't try to draw every branch. Draw the general shapes, and note where the main branches are, where they cross, and where the trunk divides.

When drawing a tree in full leaf, draw the main shape first, then add leaves in places to give the character of the tree. Keep the line flowing, working all over the tree continuously.

You could try detailed studies of part of a tree, such as the trunk with all the knots, the pattern of the bark, lichen and fungi. Sometimes roots are exposed, revealing interesting textures and patterns.

When tackling groups of trees, treat them as one mass, and add shadow to suggest the forms of some individual trees. Add one or two trunks, which may be set at different angles or massed together, but don't put in a trunk under every tree.

Don't put in foliage as a solid shape. Leave some

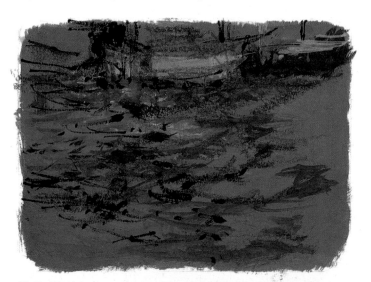

Reflections in gouache, crayon and pastel over an underlying grey wash. Gouache was used to create a zigzag pattern, which was accented with blue crayon. This lively rendition gives a feeling of movement and broken reflections on the water.

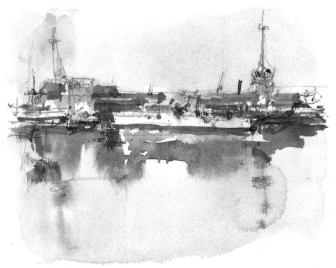

In contrast, watercolour has been used to describe a still, calm surface. The shapes of the boats are mirrored quite clearly in the water, and the watercolour wash has been used with hard edges in places to emphasize this.

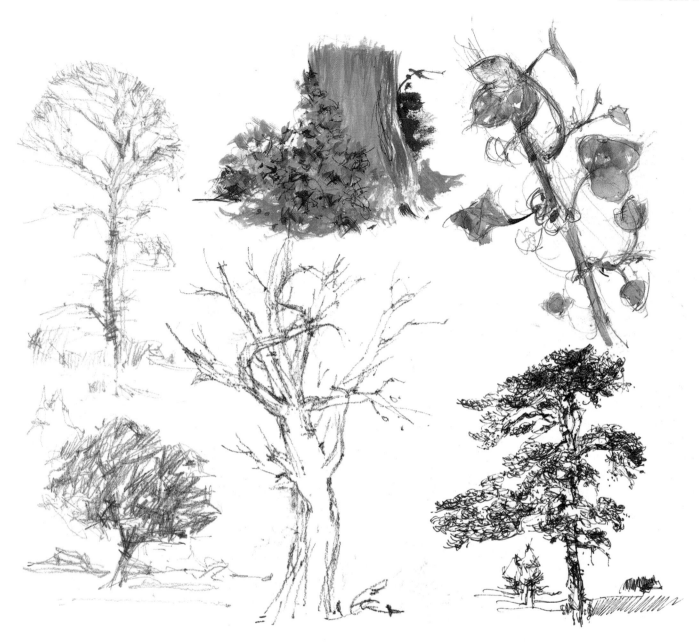

highlights. If working in colour, observe what type of green the foliage is – whether dark or light, and whether it has orange, red or yellow tinges. Drawings of individual leaves will give you a guide to the range of colours in a particular tree. Feel free to interpret the overall scene by varying the colours that you use.

Keep a sketchbook for trees, and study their shapes, relative sizes, how they appear on the horizon or on the side of a hill. Study the textures of trees and experiment with ways of describing this. Trunks can be stippled or sponged. A whole tree can be sponged in, with drawing added on top.

Each tree has its own character, which can be conveyed by the medium you use. Blue crayon was used to draw the main shape of the tree with hatching to indicate the tracery of the branches. Pencil was used to give the overall bulk of the tree, with vigorous lines indicating foliage and shadow. Conté was used to describe the outline of a bare tree, creating the forms with line alone. Pen was used with a circular movement to suggest the main shapes of the foliage. The detail of the tree trunk and ivy was done in gouache with some pen drawing, concentrating on giving an impression of the bark. Shadow creates the overall form of the trunk. The detail of the ivy was done in pencil and wash.

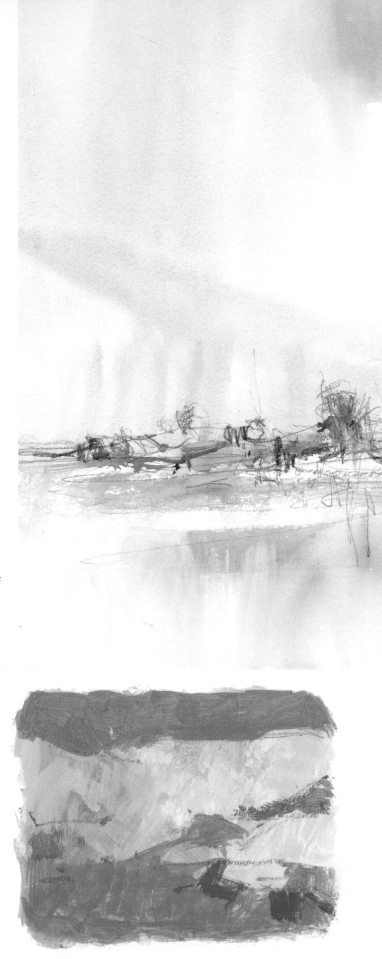

OPEN LANDSCAPE

Simplify the scene you are drawing by breaking it
down into areas based on cloud, clear sky, horizon
and foreground. If you want a dominant sky so that
you can concentrate on effects such as tightly
packed clouds, a sunset or an approaching storm,
position the horizon low in the drawing. If you want
to emphasize features in the landscape such as a
pattern of fields or hills, place the horizon high and
include just a glimmer of sky. In this case, keep the
sky close in tone to the landscape so that it does not
create a strong contrast. Don't place the horizon
half-way up the picture, as this will result in an
uninteresting drawing.

Fix the scene in your mind, and note which
clouds are moving and where they are. Put them in
as quickly as possible because they are always
changing. Next establish the position of shadows
and get them in because they can alter in quite a
short space of time. Then you can move on to the
more stable elements such as trees and buildings.

It is important to knit together the sky, distance
and foreground into an overall scene, and this is
done by treating all the elements in the same style.
Toned paper will also provide unity across the whole
drawing. With toned paper, you only need to add
accents using pencil, colour pencil, charcoal or
conté to suggest the sky, horizon, hills, buildings
and so on, and the paper will create the forms.

Pencil is ideal for making quick notes because you
can get down the shapes of clouds, the horizon line
and positions of shadows quickly. Charcoal and
conté are good for the same reasons, and can create
overall shadows and tones quickly. Conté and
charcoal also allow you to work in a broader way,
and are good for simplifying a landscape into
abstract shapes.

Watercolour is ideal for landscapes because it is
one of the quickest mediums to work with for
capturing the fleeting effects of light, skies and
weather conditions.

It is also possible to work fast in gouache. Try
using it in a reverse way to watercolour. Prepare the
paper or board to work on in advance with quite a
dark overall wash, and see how effective it is when
you put in a lighter sky over it. Once the main sky

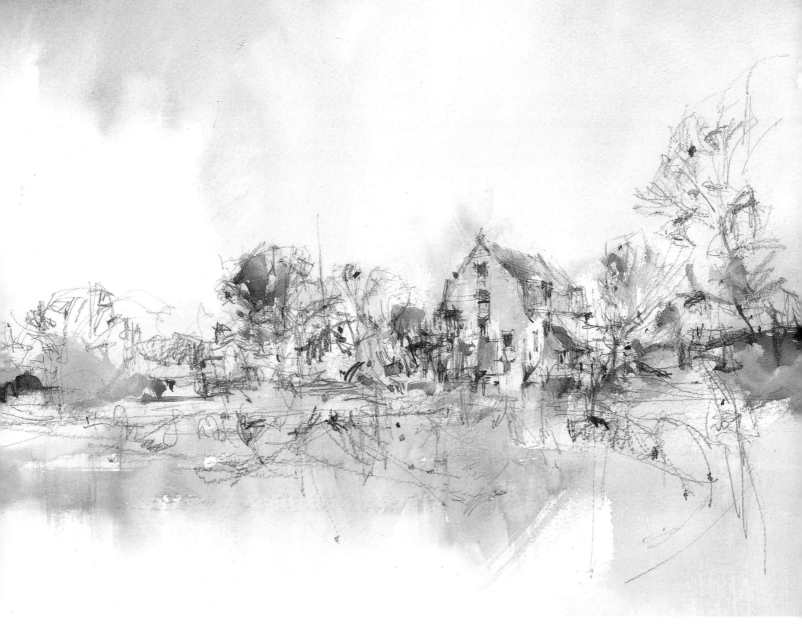

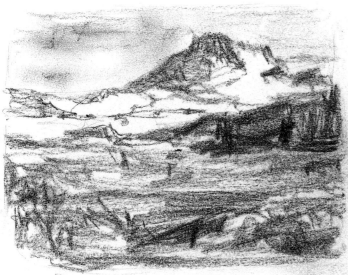

Above, the middle-distance features – the line of trees, the mill and their reflections – were put in first in pencil with a flowing, continuous line. A very soft wash was put in for the sky to give some tone, and a simple wash was put in for the foreground, which was otherwise left empty. Touches of colour were added in the middle distance.

Far left, this scene has been massed into three bands of colour: one for the sky; one for the hills, which is broken by a diagonal line; and one for the foreground. The same colour has been used for the sky and foreground shadow. Texture has been created with the paint, which relieves the simple pattern.

Left, this landscape with a hill was done with charcoal. The sky was smudged, and the rest of the scene was drawn using charcoal with texture and line. Strong horizontal lines describe the foreground.

shape is in, the foreground will automatically come into key. Gouache is also good for overpainting areas of a drawing and for adding details.

SEASONS

Working out of doors can be difficult because you have to contend with intense light, cold, wind and rain, but it is worth the discomfort because the different seasons and weather conditions are all worth capturing.

Spring is one of the most attractive times of year. There is a combination of clear, bright light and quickly changing weather. Trees are turning from winter to summer, but you can still see the underlying framework of trunks and branches. Pen with washes is a good technique to use for trees at this time of year. In summer the colours and shadows are stronger. If you are working in colour, be careful not to use too much green. Subdue the greens and add warmth to them. You can get away with using a bright palette at this time of year.

In autumn, the landscape is full of changing shapes and rich colours. Use autumn colour discreetly because it is more effective to use small dashes of bright colour than to make the whole scene bright. In winter, many more features in the landscape are revealed because the trees have lost their leaves. Because you will probably only have a limited time due to the cold weather, use charcoal, conté or pencil.

WEATHER CONDITIONS

For misty effects, use charcoal or pastel and smudging, or watercolour on damp paper. Gouache can be used with thin washes. Frost and snow scenes are best done in monochrome. To capture bright summer light, use shadows for describing forms, or work against the light, which gives strong contrasts and luminosity. On heavy overcast days, keep the range of tones close, and notice that there are no shadows. Add grey to all your colours if using them. It can be better to sketch on a grey day than on a bright, sunny one, because you can see more of the linear qualities in the subject than when they are in shadow.

DO'S AND DONT'S

Do draw sections of the landscape, rather than attempting a large overall scene.

Do decide whether you want to concentrate on features or seasonal effects before you begin.

Don't feel tied to using the colours you see.

Don't try to draw in every leaf in foliage. Go for the overall shapes in places.

An impressionistic view of autumn trees done in gouache, pastel and pencil. The style was kept very open and broad, with emphatic use of brushed dots for the foliage. Purple pencil was used on the trunks and branches. Blues and purples were used to exaggerate the glow of the orange, and the whole effect is steadied by the fact that it was done over a cream/grey background wash.

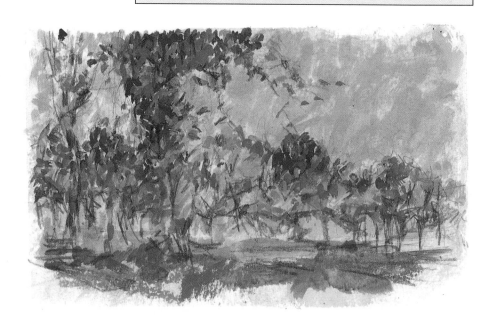

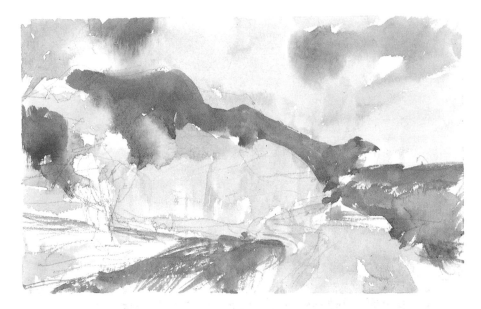

Soft washes were used to create a clear, summery effect. Creams and beiges were used in the sky with touches of purple. The whole scene was drawn with a brush over simple pencil guidelines.

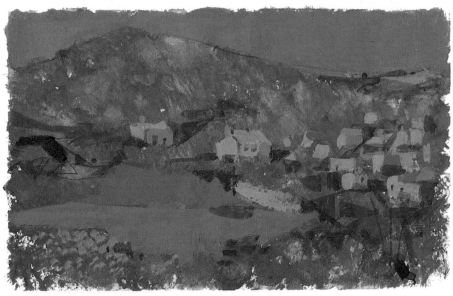

This wintry scene was done over a textured background prepared by laying a wash and removing some of it again with a cloth while it was still damp. The colours, particularly the brown sky, were used to give the feel of a heavy, oppressive day. The sky was put in with opaque colour over the background, as were the water and buildings.

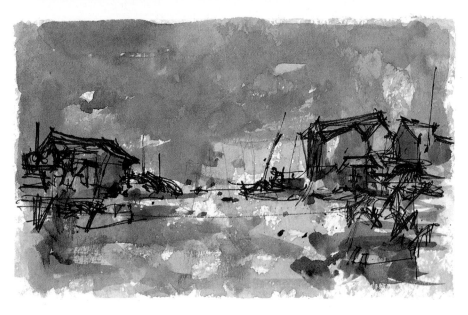

This wintry evening scene was done in pen and watercolour, with muted colours and a lot of dry-brush work. A total of four colours was used and heavily mixed. A cream/beige background was applied all over. A stronger grey/brown wash was applied over it for the sky. The strong shapes of the huts and boats were then drawn in over the top with a pen.

Practice

It is important to decide what your aim is before starting a landscape: whether you are going to concentrate on the sky or the land, or a combination of the two; and whether you are going to make a study of the features, a general view, or go for an impressionistic effect. Don't search for the perfect view; just make yourself comfortable and start drawing. If several aspects of the scene interest you, make a series of sketches. Look for the shapes, patterns and the overall tone, and remember to simplify the scene. If you want to include buildings, select one or two and forget about the rest. Whatever technique you are using, lightly draw in the main shapes in pencil before you start.

This is an exercise in using the minimum number of washes. Select three colours (a red, yellow and blue), establish the horizon and outline the main shapes lightly in pencil. Dampen the surface of the paper, and create all the features with a brush, mixing the three colours as you go along. Here, the yellow in the sky, the most brilliant colour, was allowed to float into the other colours. Then, as the paper dried, the foreground was brushed in with stronger colours.

Choose an interesting stretch of land for a drawing with a high horizon, and try to create a tonal balance between the landscape and the sky. Establish all the areas of the drawing in a narrow range of tones, including the sky area. Draw in one or two features in light and dark tones to give the scene some structure.

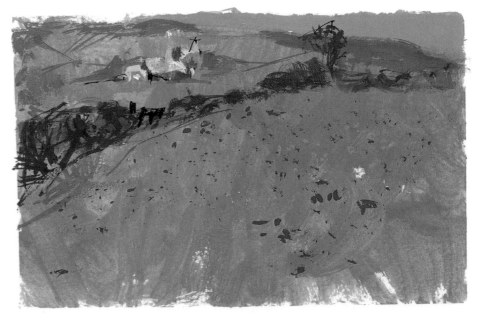

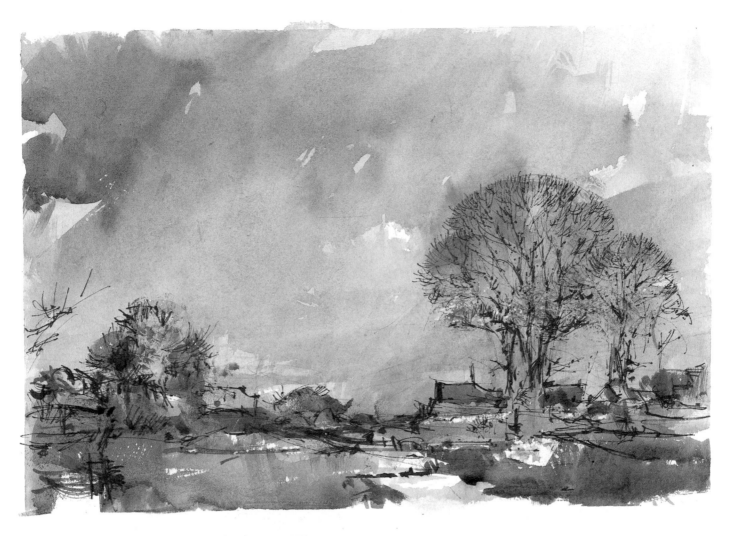

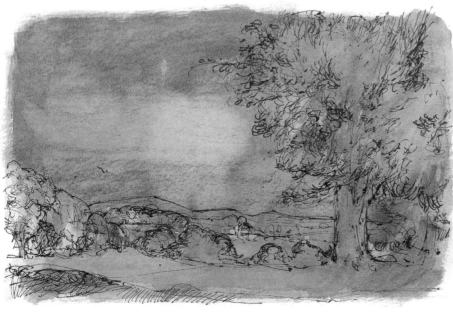

Above, try a winter scene in pen and wash. Apply an overall wash in yellow/ beige, but break it in places to create a pattern of tone. Draw in any features such as trees and buildings, and then apply a further wash of grey, red and umber over the sky. Add a darker wash of the same colours over features and foreground shadows, and then draw more strongly in places to emphasize shapes and textures.

Left, create a tinted drawing. First put down a watercolour wash in ochre/beige, blue/grey or pink/grey. When it is dry, wash it back with a brush and clean water to create a soft, vignetted effect. Work over the wash in pen, strengthening the drawing in places with a double line.

95

Beside the Sea

Holidays present plenty of opportunities and a variety of ready-made subjects for drawing. For example, sitting on the beach you are surrounded by interesting patterns, colours and shapes provided by striped deckchairs, windbreaks, coloured umbrellas, boats and beach-huts. You also have a good chance to practise figure drawing, because people sunbathing or reading on the beach tend to lie or sit in the same position for quite a long time. And there are also plenty of groups and individual moving figures to tackle.

Other interesting subjects include harbours and moorings, people fishing, piers, general seascapes and details such as lobster-pots and seagulls.

Colour pencils, pastels, gouache and watercolour are all good materials to use. And you should always wear a hat, not only to prevent sunburn, but also to protect your eyes from glare, which can be very strong near water.

COLOUR

Seaside scenes provide an opportunity to use a full range of colours. However, whatever materials you are using, you won't be able to match the intensity of colour that is produced by the strong, clear light by the sea, so you need to condense the tonal range and go for intensity of colour in your drawing.

Notice the way that shadows are often not dark colours, but contain lighter, reflected colours from the things around them and blue from the sky.

SKIES

Peculiar effects occur in skies by the sea. Although you may think the sky is lighter than the sea, on many occasions it is darker, and you can use this to make the sea sparkle in a drawing. Evening is a good time to draw the sea because outrageous colours can occur in the sky at this time of day, and are matched by compatible colours in the sea.

WAVES

Try to view the sea as a pattern, fix that pattern in your mind and then draw it. If you are sketching

Below left, a pencil sketch of the sea. Parallel lines were used in the sky, a heavier line was added to indicate the horizon, and the direction of the line was then used to create the curved forms of the waves, leaving white paper for the foam.

Below, the sea area and breakwater were masked out, and colour was splattered on to the beach area and allowed to dry. Watercolour was used to brush in the breakwater and the direction of the waves, and was allowed to run into the splatter to unify the different areas.

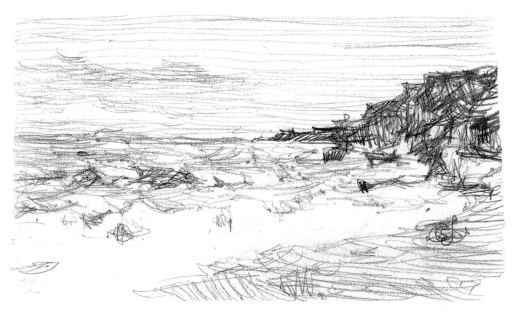

The atmosphere of a hot day has been created without using any very bright colours. Instead, the tones were kept close and everything was painted in a soft, hazy way. The strong, heavy sky is oppressive, which creates the impression of heat.

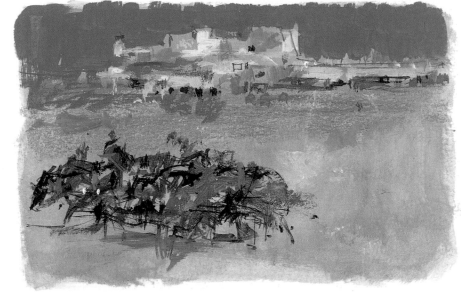

Heat and sunlight are created by bright colours and strong shadows used against each other. Shadows are directly beneath the objects casting them, which indicates midday. In the foreground an impression of donkeys was created rapidly, with accents of shadows that give tonal value to the sandy background.

Below right, pencil, crayon and gouache. The waves were brushed in, and touches of pen work and blue crayon were added to accentuate one or two of them.

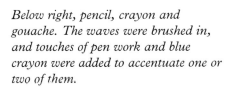

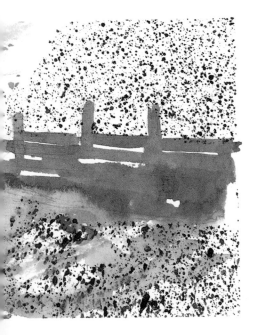

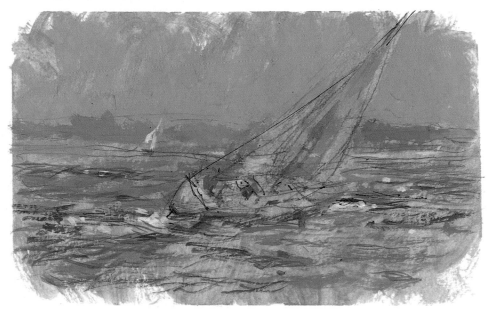

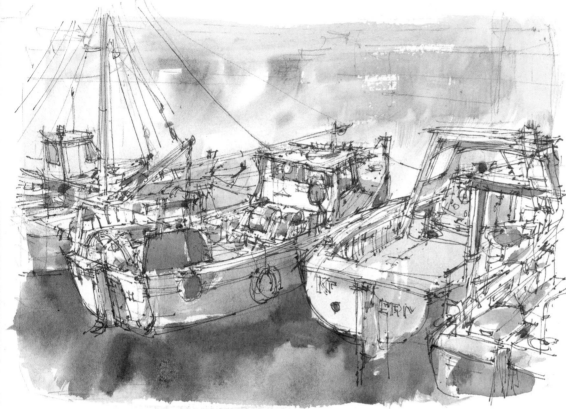

A viewpoint was chosen looking down on to the boats, which were rapidly sketched with pen. The angles and positions of the masts and the angles of the boats were studied against one another. Only the essential shapes have been drawn, ignoring the boats in the background.

with pencil, select just a few waves to include, don't try to put them all in, and use the white of the paper for the crests of the waves and foam. Because waves are rolling along continuously, you have to decide where you want a wave within the composition and then draw it in, forgetting that it has moved.

BOATS

When sketching boats, watch out for the tide, because as it goes out the boats will drop down in relation to the rest of the scene. Check the times of the tide so that you know how long you can spend on the drawing. Pick a position, set up, and ignore anyone who comes to look at what you're doing.

There are no set proportions to a boat, but it is important to get the proportions right on the one you are drawing. Don't be afraid to measure the height of the mast compared to the length of the boat in order to establish the proportions. Be aware of parts of the boat that remain parallel, such as the internal structure of an open boat, as you draw it. If a moored boat is moving, it will keep returning to the same position. Decide at what angle you want to draw it, and each time it returns to that position you can work on it a bit more.

Boats are often moored together, in which case draw them in relation to each other, and include trailing ropes, car-tyres slung over the sides, names or numbers on the boats, and any other details that link the boats or provide interest. When tackling a mass of boats, only draw the essential shapes, although you can exaggerate one or two details.

DO'S AND DONT'S

Do view the surface of the sea as a pattern and concentrate on drawing that.

Do use light/dark contrast to create the effect of sparkling sunlight.

Do use colours of the same tonal value throughout a drawing to create the impression of oppressive heat.

Don't put in every wave in the sea, just suggest their general direction.

Don't make shadows too dark.

Don't put in all the details on boats, just include those that are particularly striking.

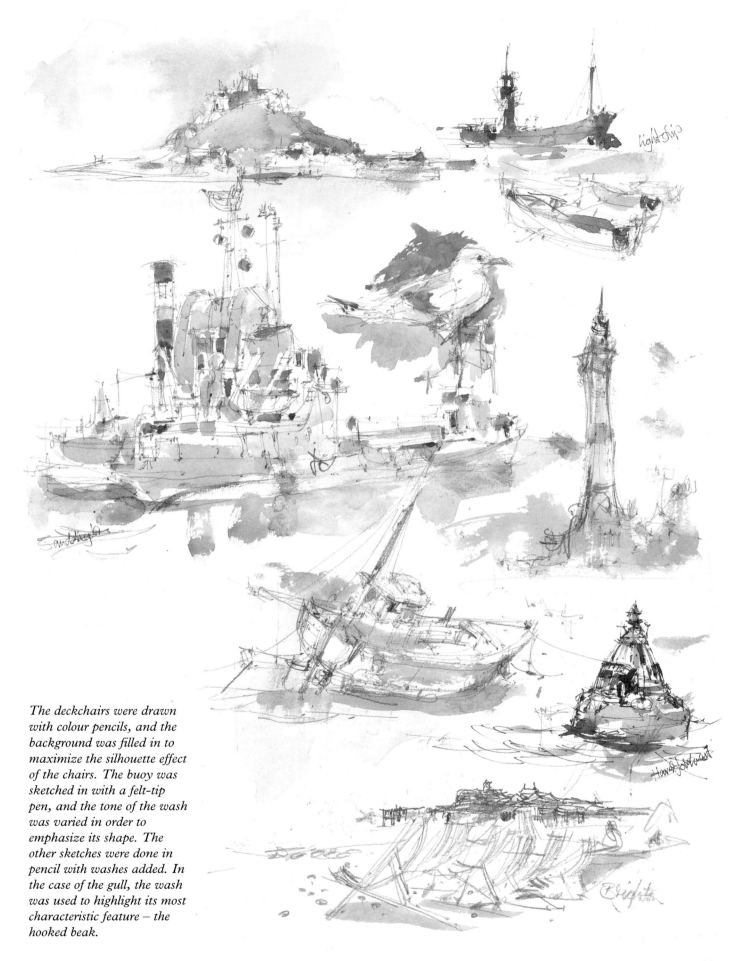

The deckchairs were drawn with colour pencils, and the background was filled in to maximize the silhouette effect of the chairs. The buoy was sketched in with a felt-tip pen, and the tone of the wash was varied in order to emphasize its shape. The other sketches were done in pencil with washes added. In the case of the gull, the wash was used to highlight its most characteristic feature – the hooked beak.

Practice

Many seaside scenes are complex and busy, and it is important to try to simplify them. The best way to do this is to forget what the subject is that you are drawing and to see it as a pattern made up of shapes. The shapes can be based on light and shadows, colour or forms within the subject. However loose the style of a sketch, it is important to study the subject carefully first, and simplify it.

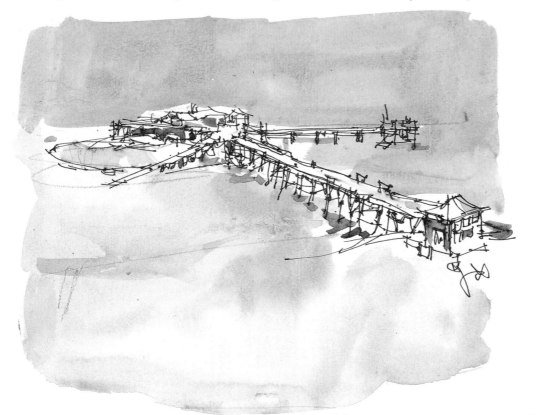

Try a quick pen and wash sketch of a complicated structure such as a pier. Draw the building first in pen, reducing it to simple forms and trying to keep the drawing as loose as possible. Add a simple wash around the drawn shapes, leaving areas of white paper around the line work. Add accents of bright colour where needed.

Tackle a more complex scene, such as a harbour, and simplify it by reducing it to a tonal pattern. Work on a wash background, and draw in the outlines first, breaking down the subject into individual shapes. Following the pencil outlines, block in areas of tone to form an abstract pattern, and add accents of a contrasting colour where needed.

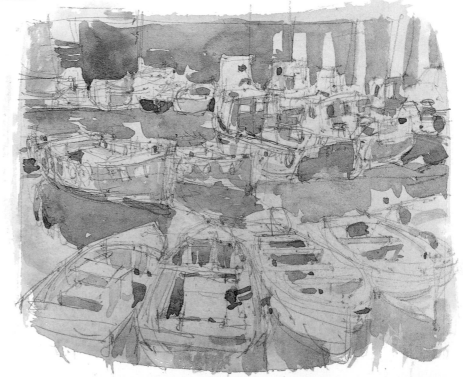

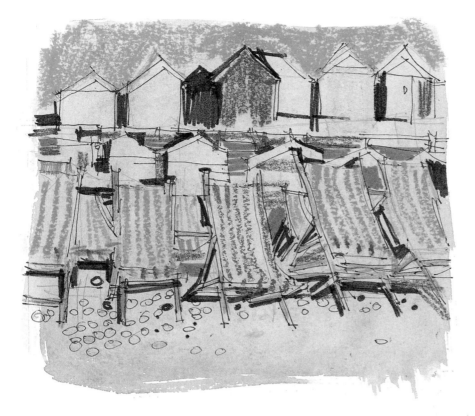

Choose a subject such as deckchairs and beach-huts, and use them for an exercise in pattern-making – seeing them in the abstract and adding defining touches afterwards. Here, the sky, some huts and the stripes of the chairs were put in first in pastel. Outlines and pebbles were added afterwards.

This is a similar exercise. Using watercolour, try to find a unifying pattern in a subject. This scene broke down into a series of horizontal stripes.

Choose a colourful subject and work in a variety of colours. The secret is to apply an overall wash first, which will prevent the eye from becoming distracted by individual parts of the pattern. Again try to create patterns, but balance areas of bright colour with areas of subdued colour so the effect is not too busy.

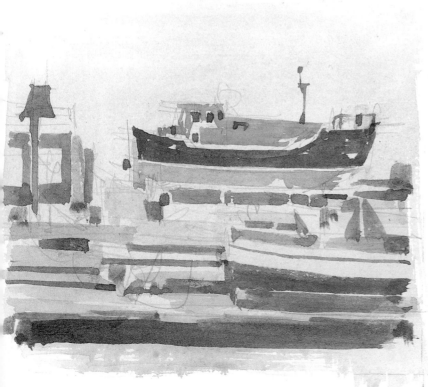

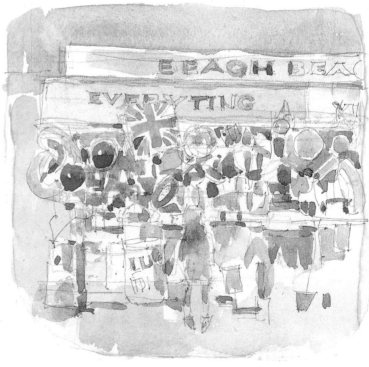

Buildings and Street Scenes

Towns can provide qualities of excitement for drawing in many different ways, although they can also look very complicated and cluttered. The most important thing is to see buildings and whole townscapes as patterns, not as individual buildings. Treat them like a jigsaw puzzle and piece them together bit by bit to create the overall effect.

The challenge lies in drawing one building against another. Try to think of buildings as blocks, as this simplifies the drawing and makes it easier to judge the size or tone of one building against another. It also makes it easier to decide whether you should use plain line or shadow. Straight lines are needed for drawing buildings. If you have a problem drawing straight lines, practise them. And be conscious of the need to keep lines parallel where appropriate.

PERSPECTIVE

To make sure that buildings diminish in size correctly as they recede into the distance, you need to understand the effect of linear perspective. Parallel lines that are running away from you appear to converge, and if extended indefinitely would eventually meet at the horizon. If you look at the roof line, the lines formed by the tops and bottoms of windows and doors, and the base of a building receding away from you, you will be able to observe this. The same happens when you look up.

In order to transfer this to your drawing you need to establish the horizon line, which is always on a level with your eye-level. If you can't see the horizon, make a note of your eye-level in relation to the scene you are observing, if necessary by holding a pencil horizontally in front of your eyes and noting where it cuts across the scene. You can draw in the eye-level on the paper to help you get the perspective right.

Everything is tied together by the perspective lines – the line of the roof, windows, pillars, doors and the base of the building. They provide the framework within which to work. By measuring and comparing different parts of the subject, you will see the effect of perspective because it will demonstrate the diminishing height and width of buildings as they recede into the distance.

Used dramatically, perspective is a very effective way of creating a sense of distance. Remember that it also applies when you are looking up at a building – the sides of the building appear to converge. If you want, you can exaggerate the size of the main building in a scene in relation to the buildings

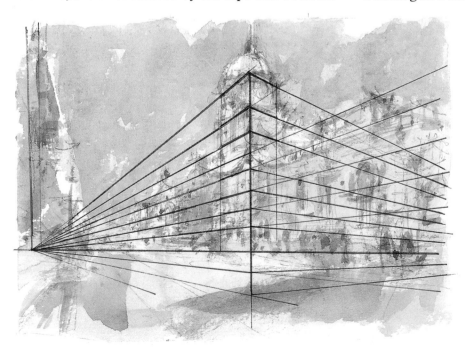

Left, parallel lines appear to converge at a vanishing point on the horizon/eye-level. Each face of a building, or row of buildings, has its own vanishing point. A low eye-level was chosen in this drawing to emphasize the effect of linear perspective.

Right, shows the relationship of one building to another. Distance reduces the contrast in size and flattens the perspective so that the buildings seem close to each other.

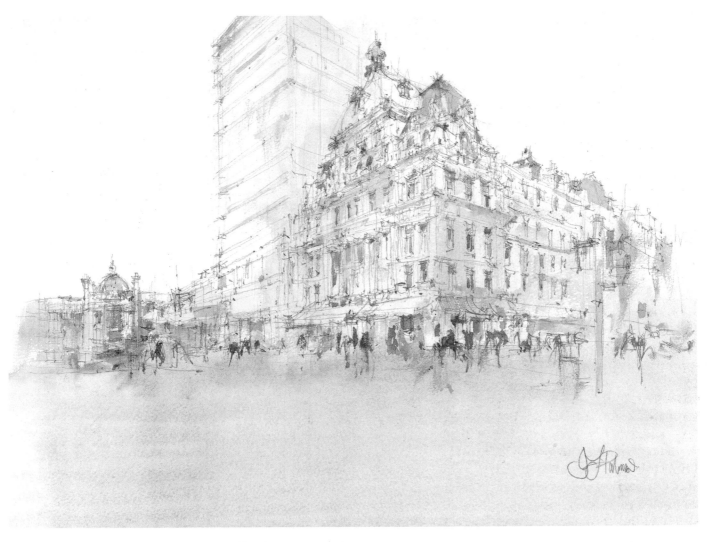

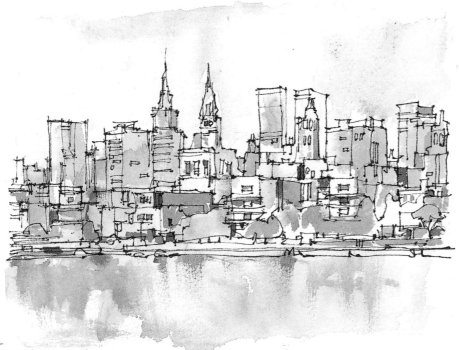

Above, because the buildings were close, and a low eye-level was chosen, the perspective was exaggerated and the angles increased. This was done deliberately to make the buildings overwhelm the scene. The buildings were sketched in pencil first. Then an overall wash was applied, letting the colours flow into one another to unify the drawing. Accents of bright colour were added to bring the scene to life.

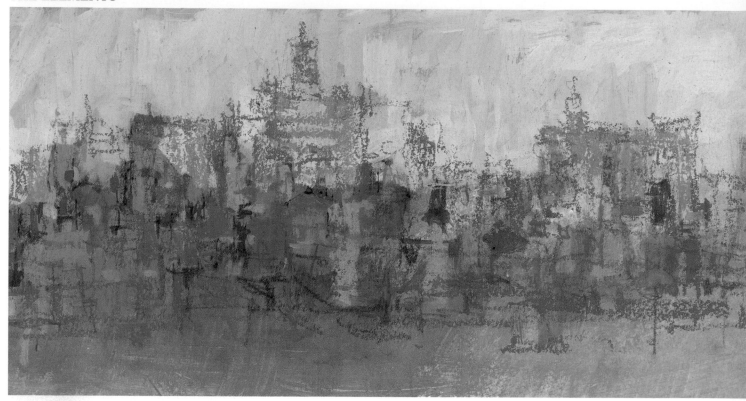

around it in order to emphasize it and to create an effect of it towering over everything else. In a distant panoramic view, on the other hand, the relationship of one building to another is not so dramatic and the sizes are therefore more constant.

DETAILS

Some buildings have lots of windows, but don't attempt to draw them all in. See how they line up in blocks, and just suggest them, using them to help define the shape of a building. Many buildings have repeat patterns, such as circular or triangular ornamentation over windows or doors, which gives the character of a building. You can slightly exaggerate details of buildings in the distance to suggest their character. However, very little detail is visible on buildings that are a long way off, so don't include too much. Note the texture of the building – brick, concrete, glass and so on – and try to give an impression of this.

Don't draw buildings in isolation from all the bits and pieces around them. Traffic, traffic lights, road signs, hoardings, shop signs, clocks and lamp-posts are all essential in creating the atmosphere of a town. If a building is being repaired, include the scaffolding. If it is a wet day, note the reflections on the road and pavement, and include umbrellas. In a panoramic scene TV masts, water-towers and so on help to break up flat-topped buildings.

Above, abstract shapes have been used to create the skyline. There is no perspective – everything was treated as being on the same plane – and the building shapes were suggested rather than boldly stated. The outlines of the buildings were drawn with a continuous line using blue wax crayon so that they flow into one another. Colour was added as pattern, without reference to specific buildings. This is a good approach for getting down an impression quickly.

Right, the basic shape of the building was loosely but accurately drawn to hold the forms together. Detail was added in places on the dome and turrets. This has the effect of focusing the viewer's attention on the dome, leaving the eye to fill in the rest. This was done in gouache, felt-tip pen, colour pencil and crayon.

COLOUR

Colour can be used to isolate one building from the others in a sketch. It can be used to create the atmosphere or character of a town, bright colours suggesting a busy place and more muted colours a dignified scene. Or it can be used to create an impression of weather conditions or time of day. In the evening, the light is often more dramatic than during the day and more unusual colours occur.

You can either make the sky light, with buildings darker against it, or the sky dark with lighter buildings – which will change the whole character of the buildings. Try both and don't feel tied by the colours that you see.

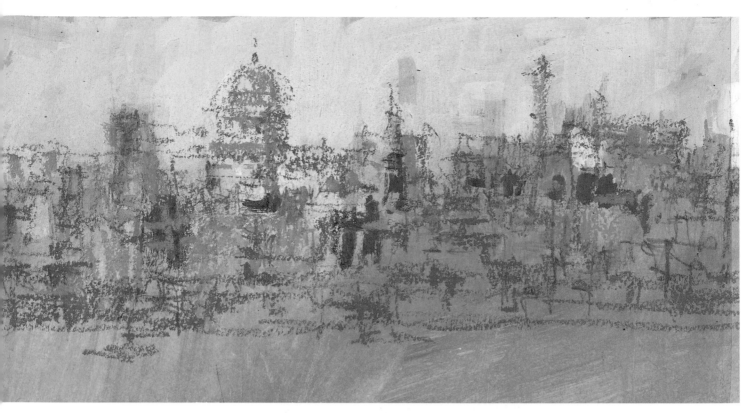

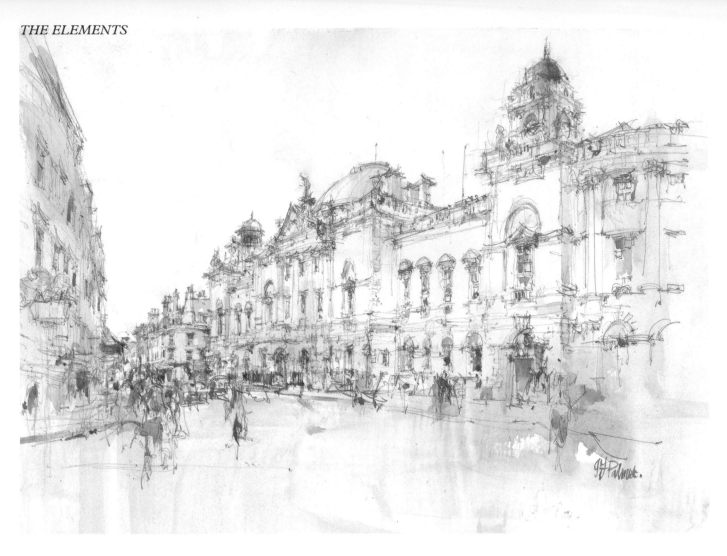

Colours tend to be stronger in the foreground than in the distance. If you soften the colour for distant areas this, combined with linear perspective, will give a drawing a great sense of depth.

PEOPLE

You can give a sense of scale to buildings by including people in the drawing. The eye-level is useful for this because people's heads are all on the eye-level, allowing for variations in height. If you draw them in from the head, they will sit happily in the drawing. Try to group people together rather than scattering them across a scene. Put them in as general shapes, don't overdraw them; and treat them in the same style as the rest of the drawing.

TECHNIQUES

Almost all materials are good for drawing buildings, but select them according to whether you want to capture the linear qualities and detail on a building or its overall shape and mass.

If using pencil and wash, draw in the structure first and use the wash to give looseness and add colour.

Above left and right, an interpretation of the same scene in the day and at night.

The day scene was done on the spot. It is quite specific and detailed, and was done in pencil and wash. The night scene was done from notes and with a knowledge of the building. A gouache wash was applied with a large brush over the basic drawing. It is much less detailed as less can be seen at night. Because a lot of detail is lost, it is not necessary to make it very dark.

Wash in the sky first, and always keep washes on the light side so they don't destroy the pencil work. If you are using gouache, you can draw with the paint and create stronger colours. You can also add crayon, pen or pastel over it to relieve the paint surface.

Felt-tip pen is good for creating dramatic effects, and the strong lines it makes possible can give the character of the building. Conté is ideal for buildings because it can provide all the necessary qualities – thin line, broad line and shadowy marks – within the one material. It also creates a nice texture that is compatible with buildings. Charcoal pencil is good for the same reasons.

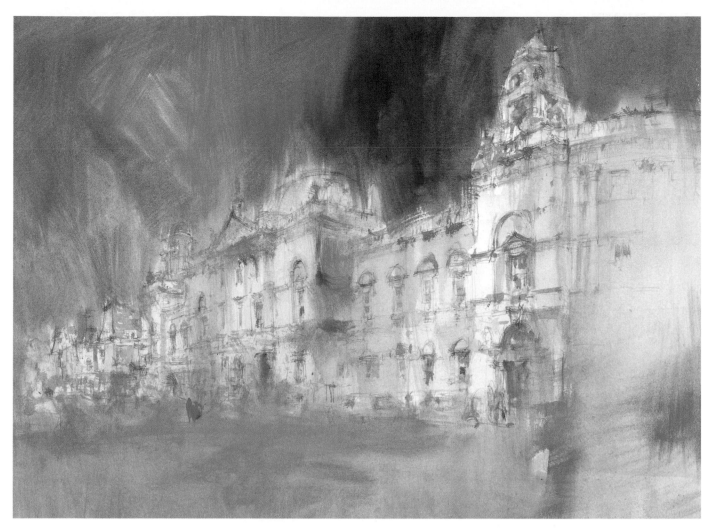

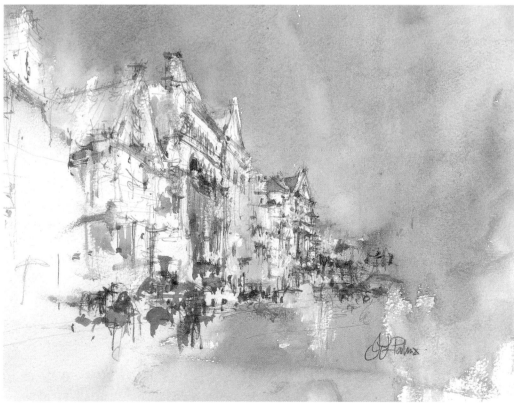

To capture the atmospheric effect of a rainy day, the top part of the paper was dampened and a wash was flooded over the whole scene around the building using two greys, a warmer one and a cooler one. Two brushes were used at once, and the colours were allowed to run and combine to create subtle variations in tone and colour. Patches of paper were left white to create highlights.

Practice

Drawings of buildings can be architectural, abstract or impressionistic, so experiment with different styles of interpretation, and different combinations of techniques. However, all will need a knowledge of perspective and positive use of pen or pencil line.

Buildings are one subject where working from a photograph can be instructive. If you do a line drawing from a photograph, you will be able to see the effect of linear perspective. Then draw your own house, first from fairly close, studying the types of windows, chimneys and doors. After that draw the building from the bottom of the garden or across the street. Try drawing the street outside, relating the buildings to one another. You can then progress to the local market, church or shopping precinct.

Below, try different techniques, such as pencil, pen, conté, felt-tip pen and watercolour wash, for interpreting sections and details of buildings. For each, select a typical aspect of the building – brickwork, chimneys, timber structure, pillars and so on – and use it to emphasize the character of the building.

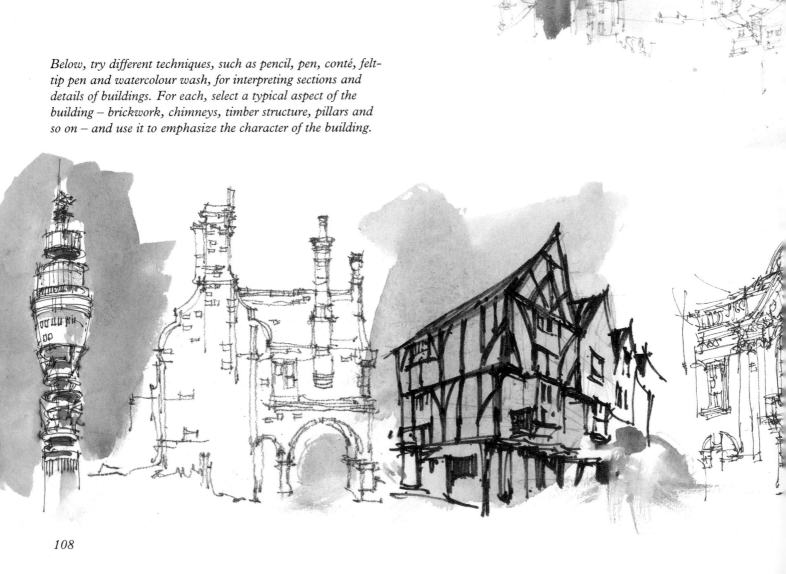

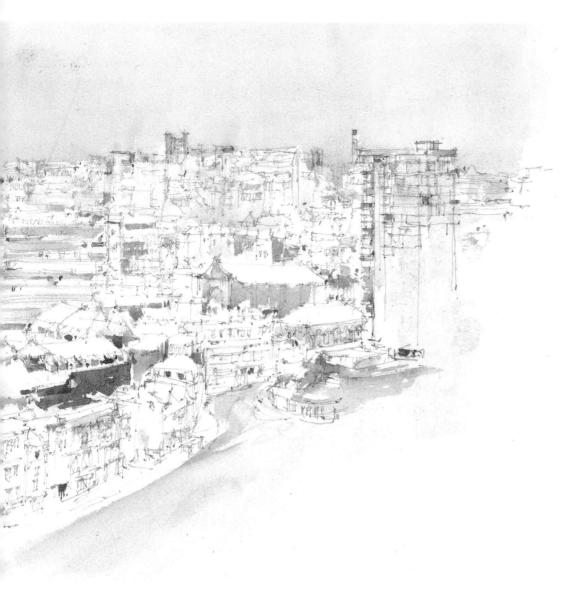

Left, find a panoramic view and use it for an exercise in pattern-making. Although it may look complicated, see it as a series of blocks and build up the drawing by putting them together piece by piece. This will provide practice in straight lines, and in using a pencil and seeing how one building sits against another. Once the drawing is established, add a wash across the top for the sky, and then add washes in bands parallel to the buildings.

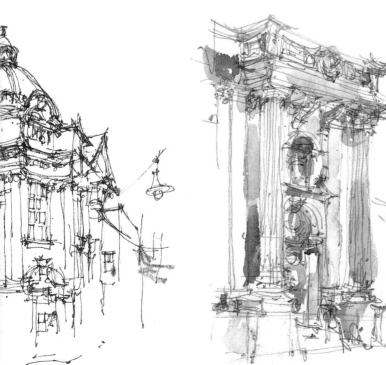

DO'S AND DON'TS

Do treat buildings in a townscape as a series of blocks, and piece them together one by one.

Do remember to study the effect of linear perspective, and the way it can be used to create space and distance in a drawing.

Do include people in townscapes to give the buildings a sense of scale.

Do use colour to suggest the atmosphere of a scene.

Don't attempt to draw in all the details on a building. Suggest them in places and let the eye fill in the rest.

Don't draw buildings in isolation from the other elements around them.

Industrial and Transport

Industrial subjects have a fascination for many people. They are functional as well as pleasing, and a large part of their appeal lies in this. On the whole, they also provide static subjects.

Everyone is surrounded by an endless variety of subjects, often without being aware of it – the local garage, for example, with cars up on ramps. Or you may find there is machinery where you work that is composed of interesting structures and shapes. Each town has its own industry that you can seek out. Docks, transport systems, factories, scrapyards, building sites, even your own car – all can offer unusual and challenging subjects. One word of warning, however: at places such as industrial or construction sites, factories and airports, and any where that is on private property, you should seek permission before starting to draw.

If you have not tackled these types of subjects before, a good one to start with is a bicycle. It incorporates a variety of elements – perspective, ellipses, angles, curves, different textures – and will provide good drawing practice.

A car is another good subject. The more character it has, the more interesting it is to draw, so if you can locate a vintage car with running plates, individual headlamps, louvred bonnet and so on, so much the better. Racing cars are also made up of interesting shapes, and are covered in foils, flashes and lettering.

First work on the overall outline of the car, getting the proportions of the length to the width to the height right. Then work from the bonnet to the axles, which must run at the correct angle. The ellipses of the wheels should be at the same angle as the axles. The back wheels are usually slightly smaller than the ones at the front. Make sure everything runs in line and reduces in size as it recedes away from you. The make of the car is best conveyed by the grille at the front.

SIMPLIFICATION

Industrial and transport scenes tend to be very cluttered and busy. If you are faced with a daunting subject, don't draw everything in sight. Break it

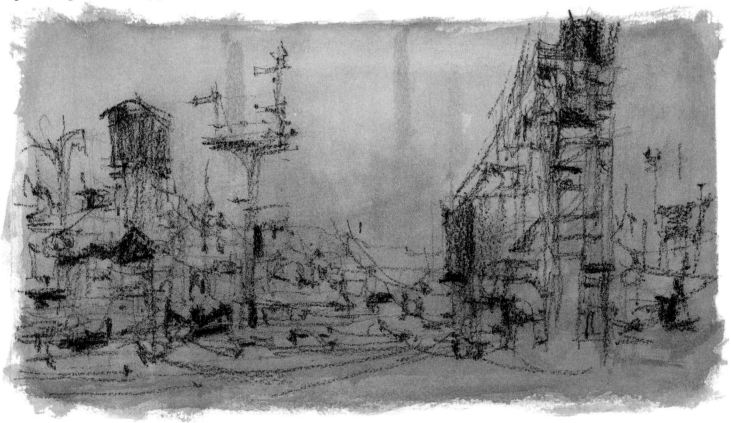

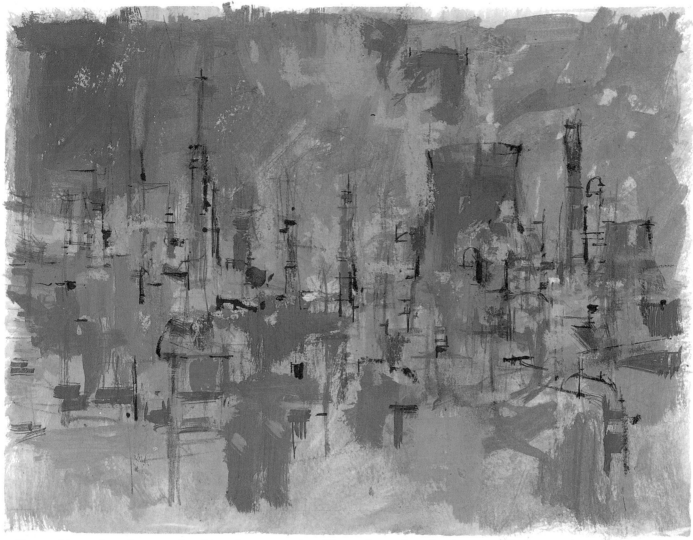

Above, this was based on a steelworks and power station. The shapes were reduced to their simplest form. Working on a beige background, an abstraction of smoke, pipes, domes and flames was built up to convey the feel of the scene, and accents of line were used to unify it. The colours were imagined rather than copied. There is no composition; the scene was treated as a pattern of colours and shapes.

Left, this was done in charcoal pencil on a watercolour background. The atmosphere of a cluttered scene has been conveyed through flowing lines and by keeping the line going to create a unified drawing. Because charcoal pencil can be used for line and tone simultaneously it is particularly suitable for this approach. It also brings out the texture of the watercolour paper, which adds to the overall effect.

down into basic, overall shapes – squares, circles and cylinders – put in the perspective lines, and simplify the colour. With any complicated subject, draft out the main shapes first in pencil, whatever medium you are using.

ATMOSPHERE
Atmosphere can be quite intangible in an industrial scene. Sombre colours can create the feel of industry, although there will be splashes of strong colour as well. If the subject is very large, put in figures to give a sense of scale. Strong colour contrasts are often present, as are tonal contrasts, and these can be exaggerated slightly. Another feature that is always present on industrial sites is noise, but this is extremely difficult to convey.

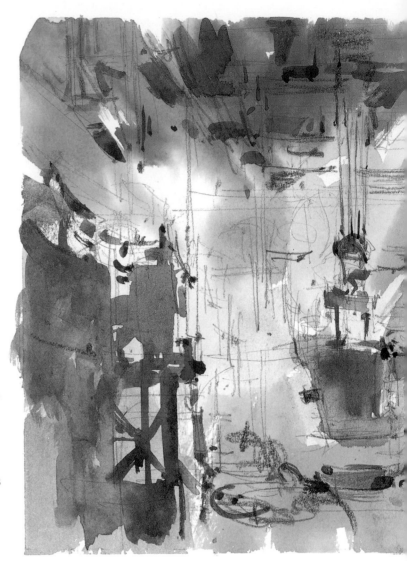

Probably the best way is to draw at speed. Busyness and energy in the drawing suggest activity, which can in turn suggest noise.

Charcoal is good for creating immediate, dramatic effects such as extreme light/dark contrasts and strong shapes, and for suggesting murky, smoky or indistinct atmospheres. Gouache is a good medium if you want to match the intensity of colour in a scene. And conté on a colour background is another good material to try.

SUBJECTS

One of the advantages of drawing a building under construction is that the scaffolding forms a framework that you can use to simplify the drawing. It is possible to use only straight lines and still get the feel of the building. Sometimes the scaffolding is more interesting than the building behind it.

Railway stations are an ideal source of subjects, both for buildings and people. There is plenty of decoration in the form of tracery, windows, brickwork and archways. In addition, there is always somewhere to sit, and you won't be disturbed because everyone is catching trains.

Canals are good because they combine boats, water, buildings, trees, reflections and wildlife. Locks are made up of simple shapes, and have interesting details such as the winding gear. Bridges were built to be drawn, whether they are stark and modern or the curved shape of an old viaduct.

Airports provide many different subjects. The aircraft remain stationary for long periods, and are ususaly overlooked by good viewing-points (check whether you need permission first). In addition there are fire-engines, fuelling lorries, gantries and extending passageways to the aircraft.

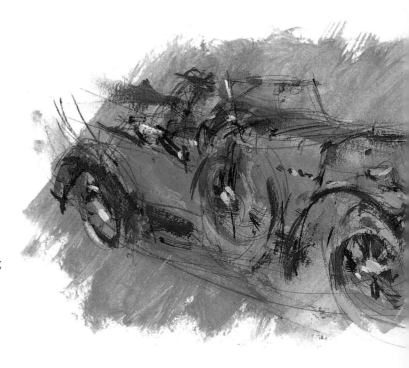

MOVEMENT

Movement can be expressed by directional lines, indistinctness, lines flowing together, broken edges and rapid, impressionistic brushstrokes. It's also possible to create a feeling of movement by blurring the background through putting it in on the diagonal. To exaggerate movement in something like a wheel, draw the wheel as an ellipse tilted in the direction in which the object is travelling.

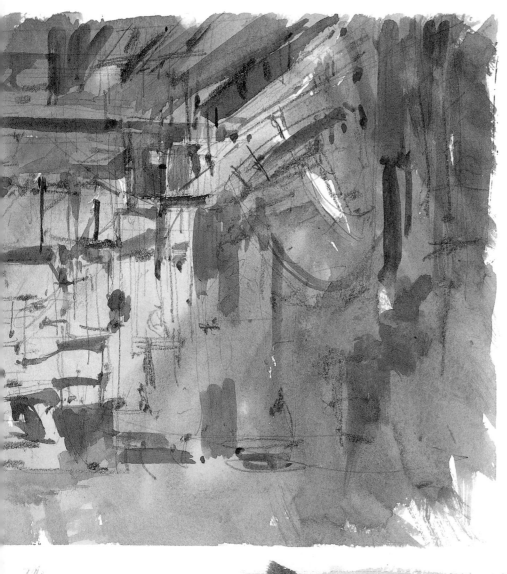

Left, a rapid, loose watercolour and pencil sketch of the interior of a steelworks. It gives the impression, through extreme light and shadow, of the moment when the furnace was opened creating a brilliant flash of colour and light.

Below left, an impression of movement is created by the vigorous brushwork and the flow of the washes, together with overdrawn pencil lines. Washes – some washed in and some dry – were applied over the drawing. Smudged lines create a sense of speed.

Below, the aircraft was outlined with overdrawn pencil lines, suggesting its shape but leaving it indistinct. Loose washes and flowing pencil lines suggest the speed of the aircraft.

Below, a pencil and wash drawing done in four stages. Left-hand strip: the basic pencil drawing – preliminary lines for the building and background and perspective lines – has been done and a very light wash applied over the top. Second strip: heavier drawing has been applied over the first wash, and more distinctive colour washes have been added on the body of the aircraft, on the windows and in the foreground. Third strip: more intense colour has been added around the wing, together with pencil work. Fourth strip: an extra wash has been applied, strength has been added to the tail, and the markings were put in on the wing.

Top right, a sombre colour scheme has been used to create the atmosphere of a railway station. Pencil work was applied first. Then loose washes were brushed on to create accidental effects for the steam. The shapes of the engine were blocked in, and some of its mechanism was suggested. Washes in the background were applied with a dry brush on to dry paper to describe the structure of the cooling plant behind the engine.

Below right, scaffolding around the building creates an interesting pattern. Pencil work creates the vertical lines and strong, loose washes have been applied around the base.

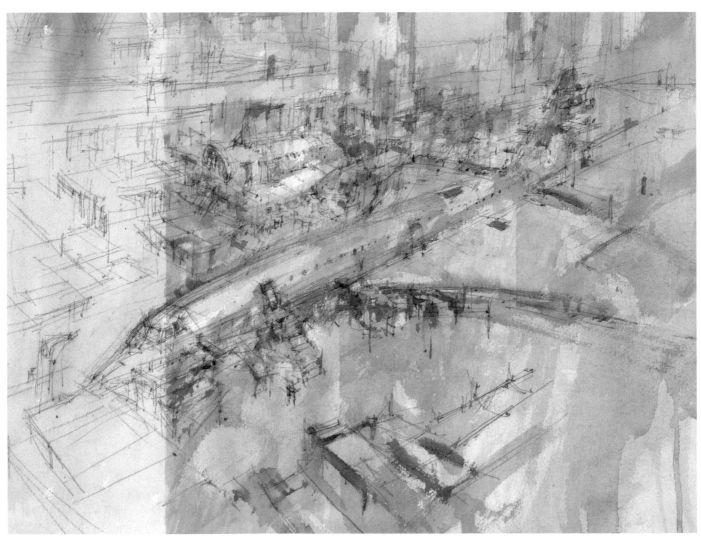

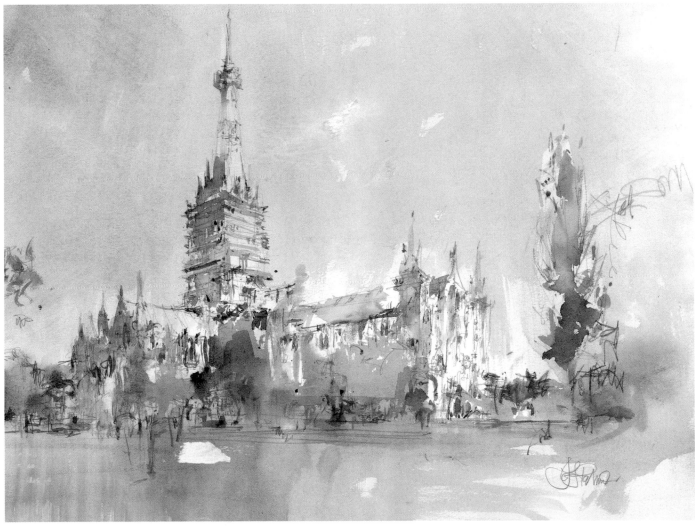

Practice

These exercises incorporate a variety of techniques. You can take one of two approaches: either you can let the medium dictate the subject – in other words, decide on your medium and choose a subject to fit it – or you can let your chosen subject inspire the medium. If the scene in front of you is full of masses and blocked shapes that are attractive in themselves, use acrylics or gouache and work in pattern and colour. On the other hand, if you have a delicate subject with linear qualities, use pencil to explore its construction. Remember to study the effects of linear perspective on any structures, including such things as railway engines and cars.

Take a variety of subjects, some solid and made up of a series of shapes, such as an engine, some linear such as a crane, and interpret them in appropriate mediums. Try using line only for a subject such as a car, creating shape and tone through the same marks. Draw a moving object using linear perspective to make it look as if it is coming towards you, and extend the perspective lines to create an impression of speed. Take circular subjects such as a radar screen, or the wheel of a bike, and use it to practise drawing ellipses. Draw the outer ellipse first and then add the central structure, creating curves within curves.

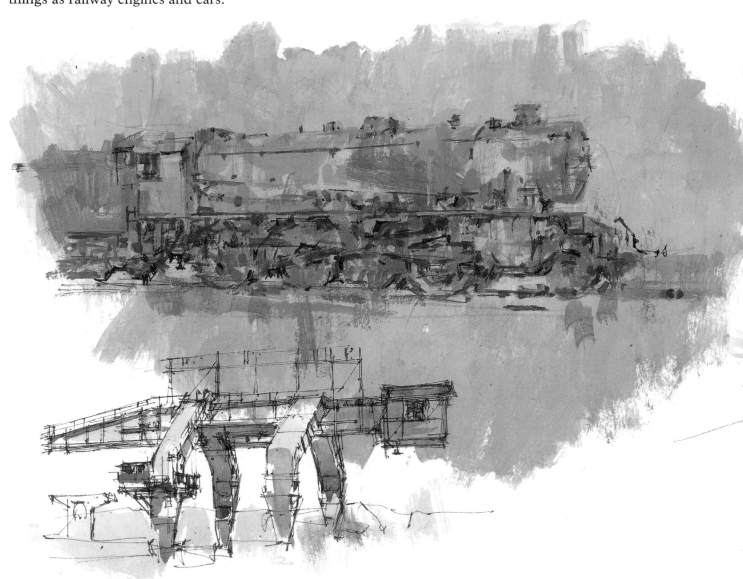

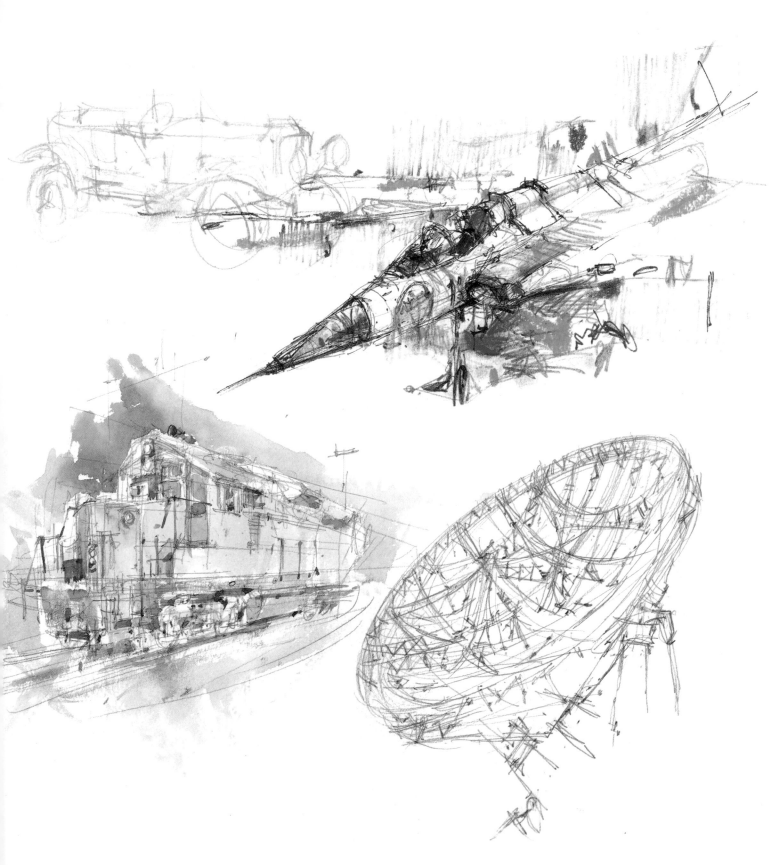

Index

A

Acrylic paint 13, 30, 32, 56, 116
Aerial perspective 44
Angles, establishing 39, 64, 83
Atmosphere 37, 40, 42, 45 46, 74, 104, 111, 114

B

Background colour 30, 56, 57, 58, 71, 83, 84, 86, 112 (*see also* Coloured backgrounds)
Balancing a drawing 58, 101
Bicycles 110
Blocks 26, 27, 46, 102
Board 30
  glossy 13
Boats 98
Buildings 94, 102-109

C

Canvas 30
Card 13
Cars 110
Cartridge paper 12, 28, 34
Chalk 18
Charcoal 12, 13, 19, 76, 86, 90, 92, 106, 112
  types of marks 18
Circular composition 50, 55
Cloth 36, 37
Clouds 86, 90
Colour(s) 56-62, 71, 80, 96, 104, 106
  and buildings 104, 106
  and industry 111, 116
  and people 70, 71
  and seasons 92
  and skies 86
  and tone 45
  and trees 89
  in seaside scenes 96
  mixing 56, 57
  selective use of 26, 27, 30, 57, 58
  warm and cool 58

Colour pencils 26, 27, 28, 32, 34, 76, 88
Coloured backgrounds 27, 36 (*see also* Background colour, Coloured paper)
Coloured paper 13, 18, 20, 27, 34, 86, 90
Composition 50-55
  and tone 46
  selection of subjects 51
Compressed charcoal 18
Conté 13, 20, 21, 24-25, 86, 90, 92, 106, 112
Cool colours 58, 70, 71
Copies 54-55
Crayon, *see* Colour pencils, Wax crayons

D

Depth, sense of 45, 106
Detail 18, 23, 24, 26, 29, 45, 76, 77, 78, 88, 104
Diagonal composition 50, 82, 84
Distance, impression of 23, 44, 102, 106
Dots 16, 18, 26
Drawing ink 22, 23

E

Edge, creating an 43
Eye-level 68, 102, 103 (*see also* Horizon)

F

Felt-tip pens 13, 22, 25, 26, 27, 28, 32, 79, 106 (*see also* Pen)
Figures 64-73, 96
  and colour 71
  and scale 66, 67, 106, 111
  drawing single 64
  groups of 66
  in settings 66
  measuring 38
  movement 68
Flowers 80
  techniques 81

Foreshortening 64
Form, describing 14, 16, 19, 26, 42, 43, 45, 65, 76, 80, 86, 88, 92
Fountain-type pens 22 (*see also* Pen)
Fur and feathers 74, 77, 79

G

Glasses 72
Gouache 12, 13, 22, 29, 30, 33, 34, 56, 74, 86, 88, 90, 92, 106, 112, 116
Groups of figures 66

H

Hard-edged wash 22
Hatching 16, 26, 28
Head, structure of 39
Horizon 90, 102
Horizontal lines 38, 39, 50, 68, 91
Hot-pressed (HP) paper 12
Highlights 12, 18, 23, 71, 78, 81, 82, 89, 107

I

Industrial scenes 110-117

L

Landscape format 52
Light 40, 42, 43, 54, 86, 92, 113
  and seaside 96
  and still life 82, 83
  and time of day 104
  lighting portraits 68, 69
Line 14, 16, 18, 20, 22, 24, 26, 27, 74
Linear perspective 102, 106

M

Mapping 58
Marks, types of 16, 18, 20

Matchstick and ink 23
Measuring 38-39, 64, 70, 74, 83, 98, 102
Mixed media 25, 34, 35, 85
Mixing colours 56, 57
Movement 50, 65, 68, 76, 79, 88, 112, 113

N

Noise, suggestion of 111, 112
NOT paper surface 12

O

Oil pastels 26-27, 34
Open landscapes 90

P

Palette, limited 56-57
Paper 12-13, 16, 18
  surfaces 12
Pastels 13, 26-27, 29, 32, 34, 81, 86, 88, 92
Pattern 46, 66, 74, 76, 80, 81, 85, 88, 94, 96, 101, 102
Pen 22 (*see also* Felt-tip pens, Pen and wash)
Pen and wash 22, 23, 76, 86, 92
Pencil 12, 13, 14, 15, 16, 64, 74, 76, 81, 86, 90, 92, 106, 111, 116 (*see also* Colour pencils)
  and wash 34
  creating tone 16
  types of marks 16
  using line 14
People 64-73, 106 (*see also* Figures)
Perspective 102, 103 (*see also* Aerial perspective, Linear perspective)
Photographs, use of 40, 108
Portraits 68, 70
Positions, assessing relative 39
Prepared backgrounds 36
Proportions 38, 39, 64, 66, 70, 74, 83, 98

Acknowledgements

First of all, I wish to express my sincere thanks to Ron Ranson, a good friend and Brother Savage, for not only conceiving this exciting series "Ron Ranson's Painting School" but for asking me to contribute "Drawing & Sketching"; a project which, in retrospect, I enjoyed.

Also, I must pay tribute to Jane Donovan, Senior Editor at Anaya, for all her help and encouragement, to Jane Forster for her very skilful layout, and in particular to Helen Douglas-Cooper, who had the unenviable task of translating my words to legible text. Helen's patience was boundless and I am truly indebted to her, as indeed I am to everyone involved in the production of this book.

Last but by no means least, thanks are also due to Doreen for uncomplainingly providing a one-woman personal support team!

John Palmer